Machine Learning for Beginners

An Introductory Guide to Learn and Understand Artificial Intelligence, Neural Networks and Machine Learning

Table of Contents

Introduction

The stage has always been set for thinkers to come up with theories explaining the rise of intelligent machines. As Philip K. Dick puts it, it is all green lights to think that androids dream of electric sheep. Well, the answer is no. Scientific facts have evolved with time to a point in space where the human imagination is full of conflicting images from science fiction. Contrary to the ideas portrayed in most Hollywood blockbusters, I believe that the human species do not face a struggle for existence with the autonomous robotics. On the contrary, the human species is edging closer to the last age of artificial intelligence. As a leaner, it's vital to understand the basis of machine learning. You also need to comprehend the challenges most emerging interested candidates encounter in the learning process.

Machine learning (ML) forms one of the major components of artificial intelligence. Machine learning algorithms are tuned to learn from existing data and information. The concept of machine learning delves in the idea that computers, like human beings, can perform their task without explicit programming. The algorithms only need to learn and advance.

In the current world, machine learning algorithms have empowered computers to interact with human beings. The machines can independently operate machines (yes, devices can operate machines), write match reports, and detect abnormalities in different systems. I possess firm resolve that machine learning at its best will positively influence the actions and production processes in most industries. For this reason, it is essential to explicitly explain the concept to enable everyone to have a grasp and the know-how on the most exciting topic in the world of technology

In this book, I will give my readers a quick trip through the concept of machine learning to impart the knowledge necessary to further advance in the field. So seat back and...lights, camera, action.

Chapter 1: Introduction to Machine Learning

MACHINE LEARNING

The thought of machine learning seems ambiguous, considering that they are not intelligent. By nature, machines perform designated tasks ranging from controlling traffic to exploring space. The various devices used today have made work more manageable and effective. However, machines lack intelligence, which makes them considerably different from humans. Through the sense of vision, smell, taste, tactility, and hearing, the human brain, receives and processes data. The neural system transports the collected data to prompt action. Resultantly, the brain sends commands to the different body parts to act per the demands. The brain stores the experience in the form of memory, which can enable one to react accordingly when a situation repeats itself in the future.

On the contrary, a machine cannot comprehend the gathered data. Despite exposure to specific information, it cannot classify or store it for future experiences. With the advent of advanced technology, developers are creating machines to solve problems that were initially meant for humans. The development of these machines involves enabling them to 'think' and 'understand' issues so that they can address them just like humans.

Over the years, computers have gained precedence as intelligent machines. They can perform tasks and solve diverse problems after encoding a set of programming instructions. The CPU functions like the human brain, which primary aim is to resolve issues. If you want to explain a numerical problem, you can do it quickly as long as you are of sound mind. With the inevitable differences in thought patterns, the chances of reaching an answer through various formulas are high. Simply put, we can carry out a similar task through different algorithms. The methods are a set of instructions that help an individual use the input to get the right output.

In broad terms, a machine uses several methods to solve a problem. A change in its structure, data, or program makes it learn, leading to improvements in future performance. Machine learning is increasingly becoming a central aspect in information technology. With the massive amounts of data available, smart data analysis will be an inevitable phase of technological progress.

But why should machines learn? Well, machine learning is proving to be an indispensable part of our society. A smart device can adjust its internal structures to produce the desired outputs after gathering a wide array of sample inputs. Besides, smart machines analyze large data piles to establish any correlations through the process of data mining. Humans can only encode specific amounts of data; with an intelligible machine, it becomes easy to capture large amounts of information.

There is resurging interest in the concept of machine learning. With the growth of computational processing and significant data volumes, the popularity of machine learning can only increase. Machine learning is becoming a vast domain as technology continues to advance. Resultantly, ML has several classifications based on the learning tasks.

Through this chapter, you will understand the growth of machine learning, its application and related disciplines, and the broad category of artificial intelligence. The other chapters will delve more in-depth on the applications related to machine learning.

The Development of Machine Learning

While the 90s stand out as the golden era of the popularity of machine learning, the concept has a long history. Before the 1940s, most mathematical underpinnings used in modern day machine learning were available in statistical forms. One of the notable mathematicians was Thomas Bayes, who developed the concept of a theorem in 1812. The theorem is vital in data science, particularly the Bayesian inferences, which determines the probability of information's availability. In 1805, Andrien-Marie came up with the Least Squares method, mostly used in data fitting. Later in 1913, Andrey Markov developed the Markov Chains that described the different analysis techniques. Markov Chains compute probabilities of occurrence of events, which is a critical aspect in machine learning.

During the late 1940s, the development revolved around stored-program computers. The computers stored programs and data collectively. The stored instructions in a computer's memory enabled it to perform different tasks, either intermittently or in a sequence. John Von Neumann introduced the idea in the late 1940s. He proposed the electronic storage of programs in a binary-number format to allow the computer to modify the instructions. Neumann worked with J. Presper Eckert and John W. Mauchly, a development that enhanced the power and flexibility of digital networks. Later in 1949, England Engineers built Manchester Mark 1, while the Americans came up with EDVAC. Both developments were stored-program computers that had increased functionalities.

In 1950, Allan Turing had a query on the ability of machines to think. He developed a technical and philosophical approach to analyze the quagmire. Turing came up with the imitation game, which sought to ask questions to a machine and a human.

Through the responses, the interrogator was to deduce the difference between a human and a computer. In conclusion, Turing believed that from an intellectual perspective, the digital machines could pass as humans.

In 1951, Dean Edmonds and Marvin Minsky developed the SNARC, which was an artificial neural network. Minsky had the idea of learning machines. Together with his colleague Dean, they used electromechanical and analog components to make 40 neurons. They wired the neurons into a network. After that, they installed a potentiometer and capacitor for long-term and short-term memory. Edmond and Minsky tested the machine's learning capability by navigating it through a virtual maze. A positive reward moved the potentiometer, which prompted learning that enabled it to solve future mazes. Minsky invented many other programs after becoming part of the MIT AI Laboratory.

Breakthroughs in artificial intelligence were bleak between the 1950s and 1960s. The previous enthusiasm in AI-related research reduced remarkably. Consequently, the funding was minimal, leading to an unanticipated stall in the field. In the 1980s, there were some changes. Researchers rediscovered old ideas and applied them in new settings. The use of terms such as computational intelligence and informatics came to play.

The popularity of machine learning increased in 1996 when Deep Blue (an IBM computer) won against Garry Kasparov, the then world chess champion. The game was monumental, not only in the world of chess but also in the development of machine learning. In game one, Kasparov resigned after losing to the computer. Deep Blue relied heavily on brute computing power to score against the champion. From the encounter, it was clear that machine learning was taking the world by a storm.

In 2006, back-propagation promoted machine learning by training deep neural networks. The concept grew in the early 1960s, but it gradually became unpopular. However, Geoff Hinton revived back-propagation through the introduction of highly effective modern processors around 2006. Deep learning has continually become central to machine learning. Later in 2014, DeepMind became prominent after the development of a neural network capable of playing videos. The technologies could analyze pixels of behavior on a screen. The Neural Turing Machine could also access a computer's external memory to complete the functions. The development was one of the notable advancements in the 21st century.

Recent developments have seen the growth of speech recognition through the Long Short-Term Memory pioneered by Hochreiter and Schmidhuber. This neural network learns tasks necessitating memory. Creation of technologies such as Google speech recognition shows the extent LSTM has been impactful. Facial recognition is another program that depicts the utilization of machine learning. The evaluation of most of the face recognition algorithms shows that they are increasingly becoming more accurate.

What is Machine Learning?

One of the earliest definitions of machine learning was by Arthur Samuel in 1959. He stated that machine learning is the inherent capability of a computer to learn without undergoing programming. In simple terms, machine learning involves the study of techniques and algorithms for automating solutions to problems unsolvable through conventional programming. The two steps characterizing standard programming are receipt of specifications and implementing the design. The specifications give the commands on what to do, tasking the computer with the design and implementation. The traditional programming has been challenging because a machine might not detect the message in the intended way.

Machine learning algorithms have a generic way of solving these problems. The algorithms learn from the labeled data and don't necessarily require an intricate and detailed design to execute a task. They learn from the data presented, and with more data sets, the level of accuracy is high. When a machine 'understands' the model of a labeled dataset, it can make precise predictions of information that is not within the set. Machine learning has a better outcome than human-created rules. ML algorithms incorporate the data points within a dataset leading to increased accuracy due to the absence of human bias.

Data has an indispensable role in machine learning. The algorithms help to discover the data properties necessary towards solving a problem. The quantity and quality of data have significant implications on the prediction and learning performance. Machine learning has improved the global economy, health, and other areas of global concerns, making it a requisite in our daily lives.

Importance of Artificial Intelligence

The use of the terms Artificial Intelligence and machine learning interchangeably is evident in many scholarly articles. Nonetheless, the two terms are different. Artificial Intelligence is a broader field than machine learning, with the latter being one of the popular applications of AI. In simple terms, Artificial Intelligence is the computer's ability to perform tasks that necessitate human intelligence. The name was coined to describe the development of systems through an intellectual process akin to human reasoning, memorization, generalization, and discovering meaning. AI grew gradually after the development of computers. Despite the growing research in the memory capacity and processing speed of computers, the technology is yet to match with the highly intelligent human mind. However, some of the created programs have high performance levels that depict professionalism and expertise in executing diverse tasks.

The improved computing power, large data volumes, and advanced logarithms have increased the popularity of AI. In the 1950s, early research on Artificial Intelligence focused on topics such as symbolic methods and problem-solving. The concept gained precedence in the 1960s when the US Department of Defense started training computers to imitate human reasoning. In one of the street mapping projects, the Defense Advanced Researched Projects Agency developed personal assistants that foresaw the efficiency of the project. Following such advancements, computer automation became prevalent. AI is continuing to evolve, and the benefit it has to different industries is insurmountable.

Artificial Intelligence is of utmost importance, particularly with the growing complexity of industries. AI adds an aspect of intelligence to products. While you don't buy AI as an application, the products you purchases have AI enhancements, which improves their capabilities. Features such as bots, automation, smart machines, and conversational platforms can develop several technologies, ranging from investment analysis to security intelligence.

AI uses automation to perform high-volume and frequent tasks. This technology oversees a seamless completion of computerized tasks with no fatigue. Consequently, the level of accuracy is high. The concept of deep learning in neural networks, makes the machines perform exceptionally. In the case of medical fields, AI performs like trained radiologists.

Through the diverse techniques in Artificial Intelligence such as image recognition, classification, and deep learning, MRIs are becoming more accurate.

Contrary to conventional computer programs, AI can analyze more profound and more complex data. The new technology uses neural networks with numerous layers. With more data, the results are more accurate. AI also gathers enough information from the presented data. In this age of high competition in all industries, using AI to mine the best data can give you an edge of other firms.

Artificial Intelligence has a broad scope. However, you can view it as part science, part engineering. The scientific goal of AI is to analyze ideas that represent knowledge, the use of that knowledge, and systems assembly. Conversely, the engineering goal of AI is to use intelligence to solve some of the real-world issues. It is crucial to understand the role of Artificial Intelligence. Many people have the false impression that the ultimate goal of AI is to replace human workers in the commercial sector. While AI has dramatically reduced the labor cost, it is impossible to work solely with computers in the absence of humans.

With the growth of Artificial intelligence, many industries are enjoying increased productivity and efficiency. Today, almost all industries are investing in artificial intelligence. The diverse capabilities in artificial intelligence have helped companies to automate and optimize their processes towards increasing profitability. One of the critical uses of AI is enabling businesses to know their customers. Such insights lead to accurate predictions on the customers' preferences and demands.

Consequently, it becomes plausible to have personalized customer relationships. Another critical area of influence is on products and services. Consumers are ever eager to have intelligent products such as smartphones, home appliances, and cars. The automation of business processes is another great invention that has made AI gain precedence.

The banking sector is one of the industries relying heavily on AI. Automatic learning, bots, adaptive intelligence, and automation have become an integral part of the industry. Some of the areas that automated data is relevant to include auditing and digitization. Feedback automation to customers' queries is also standard. In essence, artificial intelligence improves the effectiveness, precision, and speed of human efforts in the banking industry. American Express is one of the companies that have embraced artificial intelligence to improve customer service and detect fraud. Mastercard is another example of a firm using AI to reduce cases of false declines that lead to significant losses each year.

In the manufacturing industry, the Internet of Things and artificial intelligence are enabling companies to remain competitive within the global economy. With the use of data analytics, artificial intelligence is providing advancements such as nanotechnology, Virtual Reality, Augmented Reality, and robotization. A company such as BMW has embraced AI in its recent car models. Tesla, on the other hand, is manufacturing smart cars; while Volvo is building the world's safest vehicles through machine learning.

The retail sector ranks highest in investment in artificial intelligence. The areas that are benefiting within the retail industry include operations involving multiple channels, purchases, and customer service. Alibaba Group is one of the multinationals using AI in its different business operations. The AI tools allow customers to navigate through the Alibaba online portals. Additionally, the company is using AI to create 'smart cities' that will promote a smooth flow of traffic, waste management, and lighting.

Artificial intelligence is reigniting the transport sector through advancements such as self-driving cars, route optimization, and radars that detect any road obstacles. The developments affect logistics directly. In the case of self-driving vehicles, operations can be 24 hours because they don't depend on the availability of a driver. The logistics sector have reduced costs and enjoy high profitability.

The numerous AI applications in education are changing the academic world. Education is becoming more personalized and convenient following the increased accessibility of educational materials. Today, online classes are on the rise. You only need a computer and a stable internet connection. The invention has made it possible to undertake a course from any region without being physically present. In academic institutions, AI is promoting the automation of several administrative tasks. Resultantly, educators are focusing on students more than other operations within a school.

With the exciting changes resulting from artificial intelligence, it is clear that technology will change a significant part of our daily lives. Recent improvements are making the advancement to be more adaptable. Further research and information are necessary so that the public can understand the significance of AI. As it stands, there are innumerable controversies because of the ethical dilemma created by artificial intelligence.

Applications of Machine Learning

Machine learning is an outgrowth of Statistics and Computer Science. While Computer science focuses primarily on manual programming, machine learning considers the 'how' of self-programming. On the other hand, statistics focus on conclusions that one can infer from specific data, while machine learning incorporates the idea of computational algorithms and architecture that can help capture, index, store, merge, and retrieve the data. Early researchers established the existence of a close relationship between statistics and machine learning. Michael I. Jordan is one of the scholars who argued that machine learning ideas, including the theoretical to the methodological principles, have their basis in statistics. Over the years, some statisticians have significantly borrowed from machine learning to develop the field of statistical learning.

Machine learning and its related fields have several applications that are useful to our daily lives. One of the uses of ML is the virtual personal assistants, such as Google and Alexa. The virtual assistants have influenced most industries today because of improved convenience. They help find relevant information any time you ask. When you activate the virtual assistant, it can help answer different queries and act as alarms or reminders. The virtual assistants utilize your phone's different apps to collect information that can help you schedule better. Platforms such as mobile apps, smartphones, and smart speakers can incorporate virtual assistants.

Video surveillance is another application powered by machine learning. It is difficult for one individual to monitor several video cameras. Training computers to control a video surveillance system is one of the surest ways to effectiveness. With this technology, it is possible to detect and deter crimes. The machine learning-enabled device can track any unusual occurrences and make timely alerts. It can detect motion, stumbling movement, or cases of standing motionless, which can signify an imminent attack. With the system's timely alerts, human attendants can act promptly to address any mishaps. In this case, machine learning improves different surveillance services.

Machine learning helps to filter malware and email spam. The technology updates the spam filters continuously. Some of the available spam filtering technologies cannot detect the tricks used by spammers. Machine learning powers spam filtering techniques such as Decision Tree Induction. The services detect thousands of malware, which are mostly similar to previous versions. In-depth insights into the coding allow ML to power these security programs. It becomes easy to detect malware because they rarely vary from the previous ones.

The popularity of search engines has necessitated the use of machine learning to refine results. Search engines such as Google have improved their relay of search results because of incorporating machine learning. Each time you engage in an online search, the backup algorithms note your response to the presented results. Your activities on a webpage make the search engines interpret it as satisfaction with the displayed results. If you continue searching without opening specific pages, the search engines assume that your results did not match with the queries. Consequently, the algorithms try to improve the outcomes and might make extra suggestions.

With the growing use of social networking services, using machine learning to improve social media experience is becoming popular. The advancement is personalizing news feed, making it possible to have ads targeting. The move is beneficial to users and businesses. The applications of machine learning are in our day-to-day social media use. In Facebook, the 'People You May Know' suggestion is the work of ML. The application collects information based on your connections, interests, the profiles you visit, or colleagues to suggest friends consider. Another intriguing invention that is attributable to machine learning is face recognition. When you upload a picture with a group of friends, Facebook is likely to recognize them if they are in your list of friends. You might get tagging suggestions. The precision concept is one of the core features of machine learning.

Increased used of cyberspace has led to inevitable concerns of cybersecurity. Through machine learning, it is possible to detect online fraud. ML is securing cyberspaces, and financial entities such as PayPal are enjoying the anti-money laundering features. The company has several tools in place to analyze transactions and analyze its legitimacy. The techniques can detect fraudulent activities and limit the involved accounts.

Commuting predictions is an area that machine learning has dramatically explored. The GPS navigation services stand out in traffic predictions. Using the service allows the traffic control technology to save our velocities and current locations. The data helps to map out the approximate traffic and execute a congestion analysis. The transport agencies in different regions can take advantage of this technology to address traffic snare in some streets. Online transportation networks have also enhanced commuting. When you book a cab, you get the estimated cost. Companies such as Uber have used machine learning to affect predictions and improve customer experience.

When you visit a website, you are likely to get an active chat box, which allows you to chat with a company's customer support representative. Most companies cannot manage a live executive to attend to everyone who visits the website; chatbots have made the service plausible. When you ask a query, the chatbot gathers information from the company's website and gives you a response. The machine learning algorithms have made it easier for the bots to understand queries and respond appropriately.

Machine learning is making significant changes in almost every sector. More research on the field is necessary. With the right information, the public will know how to explore machine learning and make the most out of this technology.

Chapter 2: Types of Machine Learning

Computers have become an integral part of modern day operations in almost every sphere of life. Teaching computers how to operate and progressively improve on functionality takes different approaches. The types of machine learning are categorized into taxonomies depending on the underlying problems or the anticipated outcomes. These types of machine learning allow the computer to learn patterns and regularities that are useful across a variety of business and health related fields in the modern world. The following are some of the types of learning algorithms useful in the process of machine learning.

Supervised Learning

Supervised learning occurs where the algorithmscreate a function that maps raw data into desired outputs. Supervised learning is one of the most common paradigms for machine learning. It is easy to comprehend. The process of implementation of supervised learning may be achieved through systems from the training dataset. The training data or examples contain more than one input and the desired output. The output is also known as a regulatory signal, which is represented within the mathematical model. An array of vectors represent the training example. When provided with data in the form of illustrations, the algorithms may be useful in the prediction of each name. Forecasting takes place in the process of giving a response on whether the answers were right or wrong. The approach allows the algorithms a chance to learn to make approximations over time that allow for the distinction between the labels and the examples. The method makes supervised learning a common option in the process of finding solutions.

For instance, the use of digital recognition is a typical example of how supervised learning simplifies the process of problem-solving. The fact that classification is useful in deducing problems makes supervised machine learning a simplistic approach that may be useful when the inputs are undefined. As long as the data are unavailable, then supervised learning becomes a rather important paradigm. When using supervised learning, there is always the risk of leaving specific inputs undefined. The model is not useful when such data are available. However, when some of the inputs are unavailable, there will likely be a problem in the course of inferring any conclusions about the outputs. The use of supervised learning presents one of the easiest and most common approaches when training neural networks.

The most common supervised learning approaches include classification and regression. In the case of classification, the use of supervised learning occurs where the outputs may have restrictions to a fixed number of values. Classification typically deals with the identification in a given data set with a view to linking new observations into such categories. On the other hand, the use of regression occurs when the outputs have a wide range of numerical values within a given subset. The goal in both examples is to ensure that machine learning utilizes a fixed set of training examples to make the necessary comparisons on how similar or different a collection of data may be in a given subset. The optimal scenarios in such data sets ensure that the algorithms can determine the class labels for all the unseen occurrences within such a subgroup.

Unsupervised Learning

Machines learning may occur through unsupervised cluster analysis. The approach involves using a set of data that is made up of inputs, which is necessary in the development of a structure. The clustering of data points is an example of unsupervised learning. Unlike in the case of supervised learning, the test data in unsupervised learning does not have labels and is not within a specific classification. Unsupervised learning does not respond to feedback but instead focuses on the commonalities. The method seeks to identify the possibility of commonalities in a given set of data and use these commonalities to develop a pattern. Essentially, this means that the goal is to task a computer with learning how to do something without providing a logical approach to achieve this task. The unsupervised approach is, therefore, more complicated and more complex than the supervised process. This method means using a reward approach to affirm success in the achievement of the tasks without necessarily providing explicit instructions on how to achieve the set goals.

The purpose of the unsupervised approach is more aligned towards the decision making process as opposed to the mere classification of these data. Unsupervised learning trains the agent to act or respond to tasks based on the reward system or punishment built over time. A computer gradually learns how to navigate past commands without having prior information on the anticipated outcomes. This approach may be time-consuming and tedious. But, unsupervised learning can be powerful because it operates from the point of trial and error, which may produce discoveries. Unsupervised learning does not consider any pre-classified information and therefore works from an aspect of the invention.

A typical example used to explain the use of unsupervised learning is the game backgammon, which is among the most complex chess games ever discovered. The original game format was outdone when a series of unsupervised programs gained more understanding of the game format and the structure than the best chess players globally by continually playing against themselves. What happened is that these programs eventually discovered new principles and approach to the game that would become a significant turning point in the game's set-up. Unsupervised learning may also take the form of clustering. In this approach, the underlying purpose is not to maximize a core utility function but to also find similarities in the set of data. The method allows for a process of developing meaning from a collection of data without necessarily having a set of pre-classified information. The assumption in the clustered approach is that the clusters set out will eventually show certain similarities that match an intuitive classification. The groups discovered may, therefore, be used to formulate examples that create meaning and develop new models based on these clusters.

The unsupervised learning approach is critical in a world where most of the data sets in the world are unlabeled. This undisputable reality means that having intelligent algorithms that can utilize terabytes of unlabeled data and make sense of such information is critical. In the future, there will be different instances where unsupervised learning will become a crucial area of focus. Recommender systems will be a vital area where unsupervised learning will be applicable in the future. The recommender system allows for a distinct link to relationships, which makes it easy to categorize and suggest content based on shared likes.

YouTube is an example of the application of unsupervised learning to support recommender systems. The approach allows the viewer to see the number of people who have viewed a specific video and offers suggestions on similar videos that these people have also watched in a bid to match shared likes. Social media platforms such as Facebook may also benefit from recommender systems as they seek to classify users within a specific cluster. Big corporate companies may also benefit from the unsupervised learning approach through the assessment of buying habits among the broad ranges of customers in the market. Unsupervised learning can assist in the group segmentation of such data to fit the product needs or the demands for services.

Reinforcement Learning

Reinforcement learning is useful when the exact models are unrealistic because they rarely assume knowledge of an accurate mathematical model. The approach focuses on how machines should operate to maximize some aspect of cumulative reward. In modern research, the application of reinforcement learning is observed from a behavioral psychology point of view. The method thus functions through interacting with the immediate environment. As we noted earlier, supervised learning operates based on existing examples. The user of interaction with the situation in the case of reinforcement learning indicates a difference between the two approaches.

The application of reinforcement learning in the field of Artificial Intelligence is an indication of the ability of the machines to learn and adjust to new tasks through interactions with the immediate environment. The algorithms adapt to taking specific action based on the observation of the contextual setting. The pattern of behavioral reaction to environmental stimuli is an indication of the process of learning that has become synonymous with artificial intelligence. Every action in reinforcement learning has a direct implication of the operational context, and this reaction provides an opportunity for the machine to receive feedback, which is critical in the process of learning. Reinforcement learning tends to rely on time-dependent sequences or labels. The results in the case of reinforcement learning depend on the connection between the agent and the environmental context. The agent is then given a set of tasks that have a direct implication on the environment. The method then approves a specific reinforcement signal, which provides negative or positive feedback depending on the job and the anticipated result.

In a simplistic approach, if a reinforcement learning algorithm is set out in a particular context, it may make obvious mistakes at the beginning. The idea in the case of reinforcement learning is to ensure that this algorithm receives timely feedback on these mistakes by reinforcing good behavior and giving negative feedback to bad behavior. Consequently, the algorithm begins to understand that good practices attract reinforcement through direct input from the given environment. This process of machine learning allows the algorithm to make mistakes, then uses this approach to assist in unlearning the methods that may have led to these mistakes.

The reinforcement learning approach is behavior-driven, which means that there will be numerous instances where the method may be useful across a wide range of fields, including in the advancement of simulation-based optimization. The use of behavioral patterns to condition a machine as seen in reinforcement learning borrows significant insights from neuroscience and psychological research where behavioral learning has been an integral part of progressive advancements in game theory and other spheres such as in the development of autonomous vehicles. Most of the computer games such as Mario may be useful in assessing the link between the environment and agent. The game allows the agent to earn points and achieve new levels in a game where these points act as reinforcement strategies. Eventually, the use of reinforcement allows the algorithm to develop a pattern, where the levels or points work as a measure of reinforcement.

Semi-supervised Machine Learning

The use of semi-supervised learning algorithms is essential where there is a small amount of labeled data and enormous amounts of unlabeled data. The method utilizes the combination of both labeled and unlabeled data. The programmer, therefore, uses both data types to identify patterns. The deduced models become the basis on which relationships target variables, and the data examples become easy to identify and analyze. The approach refers to semi-supervised learning because it utilizes data from labeled and unlabeled examples and still makes sense out of this information. Semi-supervised learning is therefore a hybridization of supervised and unsupervised learning approaches. Semi-structured data is used in this case because it does not obey the formal structuring of data models. The tags and other indicators used in the semi-supervised approach aids in the separation of semantic elements. This is essential when there lacks enough examples to develop an accurate model. Semi-structured models often make critical sense when there is a lack of adequate resources and limited capacity to increase the available data examples.

Scholars indicate that the semi-supervised learning approach presents a win-win situation in a wide range of functional fields that include the webpage classification and speech recognition fields of study. The use of this approach has been approved by scientists across the board, a more recent affirmation is within the field genetic sequencing. The use of semi-supervised methods allows for the recognition of the nature of specific webpages in a given context even when such labels are unspecified in the existing human-inputted labels. The fact that these approach allows for the inclusion of both labeled and unlabeled data increases the chance of effectiveness and utilization across a wide range of operational contexts and domains. The ability to increase the training data by utilizing both data sets is therefore a critical advantage in the use of this technique.

The approach allows for the labeling process of the defined data, then it uses the trained model to classify the other data based on the specific model. In some instances, you may find situations where you have a wide range of data with a known outcome, yet also have another set of data that is unidentified. The use of semi-supervised machine learning allows the process to utilize the known data models to build a sequence that can be effective in the course of making labels for the rest of the data sets. As a result, when compared to other models, this approach provides the best option because it is time-saving and also reduces drastically the overall resources used towards achieving the intended outcome.

The creation of an appropriate function when using semi-supervised approaches may be a critical solution in a modern setting where unlabeled data is likely to supersede labeled data in the process of classification. The use of semi-supervised methods in spam identification and detection from standard messages is the most realistic example in the modern world. The use of human knowledge to sieve through such messages would otherwise be impossible to achieve. Using semi-supervised techniques helps in resolving the high dimensionality concern that often affects the process of classification.

One of the most common methods in semi-supervised learning is the use of self-training approaches. The technique allows the class to undergo through a process of learning using a small labeled data set at the initial stages. The classifier obtained from the research is then used to classify a wide range of unlabeled data. Nonetheless, there is still a significant concern associated with the need to address the issue of deciding on highly consistent predictions. The second technique useful in the semi-supervised processes is the generative models. The model operates based on a repetitive approach where unlabeled samples are the heart of the process. The technique demonstrates a higher acceptable performance in the case of the models from this information as opposed to models that are a result of trained examples. Repetitive techniques conventional in the generative method include the interactive training approach.

The third common approach when applying the semi-supervised algorithm is the co-training method, where only a tiny percentage of the data is labeled. The context often has a considerable portion of unlabeled data, which may complicate the process of classification. The techniques allow for the running of a varying rating for each view using labeled samples. When applying the semi-skilled learning technique, one may also utilize the margin-based method. The method focuses on expanding the support vector machine, which may have a significant impact on the reduction of the overall margin costs. Semi-supervised learning can present a critical opportunity to cut on cost and reduce the time used up in the process of classification. An example of this progressive success is the recent discovery of deep learning, which will, in effect, address all the underlying problems associated with semi-supervised learning.

The best approach when dealing with semi-supervised models would be to understand the faults in each option. The self-training method is the simplest because it may be useful in almost all of the classifications. Most of the semi-supervised hardliners opine that this iterative approach is virtually universally accepted when dealing with classifications. The only limitation to this approach is that it fails to offer much information when it comes to convergence. The reality is that self-training may strengthen errors, an issue that may affect the effectiveness of the option. Generative models can offer some of the most reliable predictions, which in most cases are notably closer to the solutions. The technique is also emerging as a critical source of solutions when addressing issues related to the knowledge of data systems and the problems that arise when dealing with such structures. However, this technique also has a question that is linked to the failure to address the inherent classification problems when undertaking research. The most common concern is the apparent limitation in genitive models when balancing unlabeled and labeled data where the latter is limited. Generative models may have an interest related to the risk of being prone to errors, especially when such errors are likely to damage the model.

Feature Learning

When performing a specific machine learning task, it is essential to identify and determine the various features that may affect the outcome. Feature learning is the set of methods that allow the identification of the requisite representation of data examples in the course of achieving the desired machine learning outcomes when given a task. A typical example is the need to identify the appropriate description of data when taking up the role of classification. The use of feature learning as a plausible machine learning option is especially critical when the data in question is linearly inseparable. Feature learning may be supervised or unsupervised, depending on the objective of the classification.

The use of representative learning to describe feature learning is appropriate, given the interchangeable meaning in both cases. The approach seeks to maintain the information in the data examples while also transforming the data in a way that makes it valuable in the process of creating meaning. The technique allows for the machine to learn and also use the data in the accomplishment of various tasks and functionalities. Supervised feature learning occurs through the use of labeled data input. The use of supervised neural networks or the multilayer perception is indicative of the use of feature learning. For instance, supervised neural networks utilize computational convenience to achieve the intended ends. The use of unsupervised feature learning can be useful in finding the right representation in the process of performing machine learning tasks. The process involves the mapping of unprocessed data into a well-defined description of the same data, intending to actualize certain machine learning obligations.

The most significant advantage that deep learning presents are that the algorithms focus on learning high-level characteristics from the data available in an incremental approach to such data. The procedure is always effective because it eliminates intransigent feature extraction. The use of feature learning in the course of achieving the set targets also has a critical advantage in that it reduces the need for domain expertise as this approach ensures that the machines can learn high levels of data mining and classification. The unsupervised feature learning approach focuses on learning from unlabeled data by developing an understanding of the low dimensional characteristics within such data sets. The model often incorporates the idea of semi-supervised data sets where learning occurs through unlabeled data sets, then the knowledge obtained from these data sets is applied to address the gaps in a supervised setting of labeled data.

The feature learning technique introduces a variety of options. The K-means clustering is one of the approaches. The k-means is applied in the course of vector-quantization when considering a set of n vectors, K is the clustering of such vectors in clusters under k. The subsets ensure that each of the vectors fit into the groups that indicate a sense of having the closet mean. The approach is used in classifying the unlabeled sets of data examples into clusters. The procedure involves the addition of k binary to each sample where these samples have the k-means as the closest to the data examples. The use of feature learning may also incorporate the principal component analysis technique. The technique is useful when seeking to address the dimensional problem, which is a common problem. The problem is notable when subtracting the data example mean from the sample data vector. The p vectors in the case of PCA are linear functionalities, which may be obtained through simple algorithms.

While this approach is the most common feature learning technique, it encompasses several limitations that are likely to affect the outcomes of linear learning. The first limitation is that the approach takes the assumption that when observing variances the one with the most substantial forms the basis for mutual interest. The focus may be misplaced because this is not always the case where the direction with the broadest range of variances forms the most considerable attention. The approach has also been seen to have a problem associated with the fact that it only tends to exploit or focus on the first two moments of the data set. The focus on the first two may often have a direct implication on the predictability of the data distribution in a given data example. The use of the PCA may also be limited to instances where the different data vectors correlate with an aspect that may be overly limiting.

Further, it is possible to utilize local linear embedding in the course of undertaking the feature learning process. The technique involves the reconstruction of high-dimensional data through the use of low-dimensional variables forms the original data sets in the course of non-linear learning. The method seeks to capture the intrinsic geometric characteristics of a neighborhood in a given collection of input data. Compared to the PCA, the LLE is a more effective technique in the process of undertaking feature learning. The feature learning approach may also encompass the use of independent component analysis. The method uses separate non-Gaussian components to form a data representation that utilizes a weighted sum within the broader data set. Nonetheless, all these techniques serve to ensure that there is ease in the determined variables and attributes in a data set, which makes it possible to make predictions in a given data example. The role of feature learning in ML is, however, underscored by the fact that it allows for the classification and prediction of data even when such data is linearly inseparable.

Sparse Dictionary Learning

The representation of a training example in a data set as a combination of basic functionalities may be achievable through the use of sparse dictionary learning. The sparse coding technique attempts to find a sparse representation of the data set as a product of a linear combination of the elemental atoms in a given dictionary. The fragments do not necessarily represent an orthogonal pattern, which means that they may as well be over-complete spanning set. The technique ensures that the signal under-representation is higher than the one of the signals under observation. The approach tends to lead an aspect of improvement in sparsity and an obvious advantage when it comes to the flexibility in the representation of the data within these sets.

The problem set in the case of a sparse dictionary allows for compressed sensing when dealing with a wide range of data. The signal recovery technique is among these changing methodologies in the course of dealing with the representation of learning outcomes. Sparse dictionary learning can be utilizable in the course of reducing the implications of multiple representations. The dictionary has to be inferred from the input data if the anticipated classification outcome will be achievable. The past approaches would involve a focus on the representation of input data using minimized components. The method has obvious limitations because it would often utilize predefined dictionaries. The modern context has, however, witnessed an emerging focus on trained dictionary approach to fit specific sparsity and flexibility needs in a given subset of data information.

The use of data decomposition and compression may also be useful when applying the sparse dictionary approach to learning. Over the years, the use of image fusion and in-painting is an observable application of sparse dictionary learning in the process of machine learning. The dictionary learning approach has been used successfully in the linear decomposition that have been useful in the conclusion of the state of the art outcomes. The technique is critical towards addressing the classification problem that has been common when dealing with a broad range of data sets. The ability to create specific dictionaries for each class makes the process of classification and application of sparse dictionary learning easy.

The classification based on sparsest representation may also be useful in the course of audio and video processing. Modern day data health care also uses a sparse dictionary learning approach as a means towards undertaking a review of medical signals. The MRI is within the conventional the medical context. The analysis of the message in the case of MRI may be more simplified when using the sparse dictionary approach. The ability to patch clean images when using the model may form the basis for the growing interest in developing machine learning techniques that embodies the abilities salient in sparse dictionary machine learning. The use of dictionary learning is favorable because it offers an opportunity to conduct a signal evaluation in detail across a wide range of tests such as ultrasound, which are essential in the medical health care context.

Anomaly Detection

One of the other critical modern day innovations in machine learning is anomaly detection. Anomaly detection relates to the ability to identify unusual patterns in data set that fail to conform to an expected trend within the broader analysis of data. The outlier detection allows the algorithms to identify events, actions, or activities that may raise suspicion by having variances from the main data sets. The anomaly detection learning may fit into three broad categories, which are point anomalies, contextual anomalies, and common anomalies. The anomaly detection approach teaches the machines to detect rare events such as bank fraud or structural defects by comparing such events based on a wide range of other similar activities. The technique has been hailed as one of the most progressive steps in the field because of the ability to pinpoint potential gaps in such data as anomalies. The differentiation indicates a critical trait in machine learning where algorithms may be useful in the determination of the data items that may be defined as normal or abnormal in a given data set.

An example of such detection occurs in the case of two-dimensional data. The dimensions make it easy for the visual identification and determination of such anomalies by assessing the possible underlying differences within the distribution, between the common trends, and what may stand out as abnormal within such a data set. The combination of X and Y variable in such a subset of data allows the easy identification and determination of such anomalies especially when the algorithms can identify an underlying pattern that sets out a majority of the data set into a specific subset. The use of anomaly detection is in the health care, banking, and accounting sectors where an abnormal pattern in vast sets of data may mean a potential problem in the system.

Association Rule Learning

The association rule learning is a technique in machine learning that establishes a set of critical rules that apply in the documentation of exciting relationships between essential variables of a given data set. For instance, the transaction database seeks to identify an underlying connection between variables that are measurable based on the association between variables. The association then establishes the rules of engagement, which exist on the premise or assumption of (if) and (later). The relationship between variables often becomes the basis on which the rules of engagement exist in a defined machine learning context. The task in this machine learning technique is to identify the relationship between variables then to use these variables as a basis on which to establish a rule book.

The association rule technique adopts two key basic types of algorithms. The first is theApriori intuition algorithm. The method is common in data mining and serves in the analysis of frequent itemsets and their relevance in the process of establishment of relevant association rules. The approach may be useful, especially in databases that contain a significant number of transactions. The authenticity of these association rules may be measurable using three standard metrics which are support, confidence, and lift. Support represents the frequency of appearance of an item in the whole subset. Confidence relates to the conditional probability that if this item is in the given subset, then the corresponding item will also appear. For instance, if one buys french fries, there is a chance that they may also buy a burger. Finally, the lift is the ratio of the confidence to the support. The following formula represents this relationship.

$$\text{support}(I) = \frac{\# \text{ transactions containing } I}{\# \text{ transactions}}$$

When developing an association rule, you need to identify a minimum support and confidence ration. The second step involves identifying all the subsets in a given data set that indicates less than minimum support. Then consider all the rules in a given subset, which indicate higher confidence than the minimum confidence. Then you can sort the rules by using the decreasing lift. The approach provides the relationship between the rules in such a subset of data.

Chapter 3: Models of Machine Learning

Machine learning models results from classification, which refers to the process of data class prediction. These classes are known as categories and targets. Classification, in this case, occurs within the supervised learning category, where the target also gets input data. Classification is applicable in several domains, including target marketing, medical diagnosis, and credit approval. The predictive modeling of classification involves approximating the mapping function from the provided input variables, which lead to output variables. Illustratively, email service providers seeking to detect spam can translate it to be a classification issue. The problem is a binary classification (s) considering the classes are either not spam or spam. The role of a classifier is to determine the relationship of input variables to a given level. In sorting emails, the non-spam and spam email act as the data for training. Accurate training of data helps in the detection of unknown emails in such a situation.

In classification, learners are either eager or lazy. Eager learners utilize the provided training data to construct a desirable classification model even in the absence of classification data. The category of eager learners works solely on a single hypothesis. The construction of the model makes eager learners spend a considerably long period in training. However, prediction takes less time. Some of the models under the category of eager learners include Artificial Neural Networks, Naïve Bayes, and Decision Tree.

Conversely, lazy learners wait to utilize the stored training data once testing data is available. When this data appears, classification takes place based on the relevance of the stored data. Lazy learners have more prediction time but less time to train. Case-based reasoning and k-nearest neighbor are the main types of lazy learners.

The models of machine learning, irrespective of regression or classification, lead to different results. These supervised learning models utilize random simulation. Regardless of the approach taken, the machine learning models guarantee prediction accuracy when they use the provided data. This chapter will discuss in details the different models of machine learning and their applications.

Decision Trees

Decision trees create regression or classification to resemble a tree structure. The input data is broken down into small subsets, leading to the development of the decision tree. The tree follows a given direction and has a 'root,' which is a node with no edges. Such nodes are a test or internal nodes. The other terminal nodes have edges referred to as leaves. For a decision tree to play its intended purpose, the internal nodes split into sub-spaces based on the discrete functions of the data presented. Each of the internal nodes works with one attribute, leading to the partitioning of the instance space based on the value of the attributes.

The leaves represent the target value. A leaf can work with a probability vector to show the probability of target attributes with specific values. To classify the instances, you navigate through to the leaf from the root.

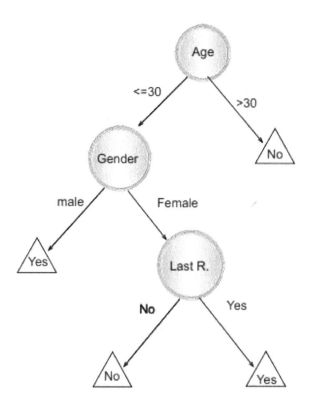

The diagram is a simple illustration of the way a decision tree works. The tree seeks to determine the probability of potential customer response to direct mailing. The circles represent internal nodes, and the triangles are leaves. The decision tree has incorporated numeric and nominal attributes. With this classifier, one can sort the tree to predict target customers' responses on mailing. Besides, the results lead to an increased understanding of the behaviors of potential customers. The nodes have labels to show the attributes they are testing, while the branches signify the corresponding values.

When dealing with numerical attributes, you can interpret the decision trees geometrically. Decision-makers use the decision trees that are seemingly less complex to promote better comprehension. Interpreting the attributes through the geometrical approach is less common because of the inevitable complexities. A multifaceted tree can be undesirable because it increases the chances of inaccuracy. To measure the complexity of a decision tree, check the depth of the tree, the number of attributes, leaves, and nodes.

The algorithms used for this model are the decision tree inducers, which utilizes the given dataset to build a tree. The main aim of these algorithms is to reduce the error resulting from generalization, leading to the creation of an optimal model. Getting a decision tree that is consistent with the dataset is hard. Decision-makers also face challenges in the construction of a binary tree with the required tests. In essence, the algorithms are feasible when addressing small issues. The methods are either bottom-up or top-down. The standard used top-down inducers include the C4.5, ID3, and CART. Inducers such as CART and C4.5 are part of growth and pruning while others take part in the process of growing.

For large datasets, the inducers for such decision trees are different. The Catlett method is one of the inventions that make it possible to analyze large sets of data. The approach works by reducing the level of computational complexity. In this case, the data is loaded in the primary memory for induction. The memory size is the determiner of the dataset that undergoes the induction. The ID3 algorithm suggested by Fifield can also be applicable because it focuses on fitting the dataset within the main memory. To increase the effectiveness, you have to partition the datasets into disjointed sets. Loading the dataset as a separate entity can induce clear decision trees. Combining the decision tree leads to the ultimate creation of a single classifier. One downside of this method is the reduction in classification accuracy. A single decision tree is preferable because it has minimal errors.

SLIQ algorithm is another approach that is applicable when dealing with large datasets. The approach involves the use of a secondary disk as opposed to using the main memory. SLIQ uses the dataset to build a single decision tree. However, the approach has a limit on the size of data to undergo processing. In fact, the dataset size has to be consistent with the main memory. The SPRINT algorithm is similar to SLIQ. It analyzes the decision tree inducers and removes the restrictions. SPRINT addresses the impurities common in large datasets.

Decision trees have advantages and disadvantages that make it stand out from other models. The benefits have increased the use of decision trees as the preferable model. Firstly, the self-explanatory nature of decision trees makes them highly effective. Besides, it is easy to follow this model and deduce relevant information. You don't need professionalism in the field of computer science, especially in a case where the tree has a significant number of leaves. Secondly, decision trees are ideal for both numeric and nominal input attributes. You can use any form of data without having to change the approach. Thirdly, the model can handle erroneous datasets and ensure optimal classification. In a situation where some values are missing, a decision tree can analyze the available data, and the outcome will be useful.

Conversely, decision making trees have several disadvantages. One of the notable methods of divide and rule utilized by decision trees limits its efficiency. The model performs well when there are relevant attributes. However, the presence of complex interactions reduces the performance of a decision tree. The second disadvantage relates to the characteristic of a decision tree, often termed as greedy. This feature makes the model to underperform in extreme situations. The approach is oversensitive to several attributes and specific training sets. The third disadvantage related to decision trees is the tendency to create complex trees unable to generalize.

Furthermore, the trees are somehow unstable, and slight data variations lead to the generation of a different tree. The fourth weakness of a decision tree is that it is impossible to update it incrementally. You have to retrain each arriving data, rendering the existing tree useless. Complementing the decision tree with ensemble methods such as boosting trees and random forests can address some of these limitations.

Neural Networks

Neural networks refer to a set of algorithms that are changing the field of machine learning. The approximate general functions apply to most of the problems related to machine learning, such as complex mapping. The biological neural networks have been significant determinants of ML neural networks development. Research on artificial neural networks recognizes the resemblance between the functioning of a digital computer and that of a human brain. However, the brain has considerable differences because its information-processing network is non-linear, parallel, and complex.

A neural network models the performance of the brain in implementing specific tasks. Developers use electronic components or simulate a digital computer's software. Neural networks use multiple interconnections known as processing units or neurons to promote optimal performance. From this description, one can define the neural network as a processor with several processing units that store experiential knowledge and retrieving it when necessary. A neural network is similar to the brain on matters of knowledge acquisition, which is from the environment. Another similarity is the presence of synaptic weights, which are interneuron connections that store knowledge.

Several neural networks are gaining considerable attention today. Perceptrons are the first type of neural network considered the first generation of the model. Perceptrons refer to computational models emanating from one neuron. Frank Rosenblatt coined the term perceptron in his early work when researching on the brain and information storage. Back-propagation is essential in training the perceptrons. The process involves providing the network with datasets paired as input or output. The neurons process data and convey it as output. Hidden neurons within a system correlate the input and the output. The figure below is a pictorial illustration of Rosenblatt's perceptron.

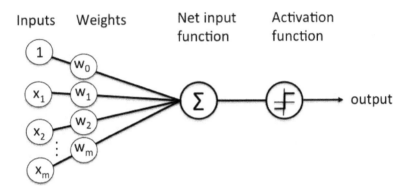

The recurrent neural network is another category of neural networks that differ from perceptrons because of the connections found between passes. The recurrent neural networks are robust because of the existence of non-linear dynamics, allowing them complex updates of hidden states. Secondly, they can store a significant amount of information on past events with the utmost efficiency. Neurons have a similar function to a computer, especially when endowed with adequate neurons. These RNNs can implement multiple small programs that run parallel to bring forth complex results. One of the major cons related to the recurrent neural network is the issue of vanishing gradient problem. The situation leads to loss of information based on the activation functions. Principally, RNNs can prove useful in several fields that require data in a sequence. The recurrent networks play a critical role in tasks such as auto-completion because they complete or advance the presented information.

A convolutional neural network is a modification of LeNet, developed by Yann LeCun in 1998. The system utilized back-propagation that had multiple hidden layers, replicated units, and a wide net capable of coping with substantial characters within a single function. Convolutional neural networks possess different features from other networks. One of the central roles of these networks is image processing. When you present the system with a clear image, you get classified data. CNN's have a scanner where data passes through for analysis. When you 'feed' your network with data, it passes through a series of convolutional layers that have interconnected nodes. The deepening of the layers causes them to shrink. Pooling, which is a form of filtering takes place to produce the final information.

Auto-encoders present another class of neural networks intended to complement unsupervised learning. The auto-encoders work as models for data compression and can encode an input into smaller dimensions. Consequently, one can use a decoder on the encoded data to have a meaningful reconstruction. The network functions by presenting the data in few numbers than its original presentation. In a case where you have 100 numbers, you can have the representation in 10 numbers or fewer. However, there is a fear of information loss, which is inevitable when limiting the input data.

Nonetheless, it is easy to visualize such data based on the ability to plot the dimensions on a graph. Auto-encoders can prove useful in pre-training neural networks, data generation, and dimension reduction. This neural network is advantageous because of its flexibility in mapping. Besides, the resultant encoding model is fast and compact. The challenge mostly emanates from the difficulty in using back-propagation in optimizing the auto-encoders. Today, auto-encoders are rarely available for practical applications because of their downside.

But why neural networks? Well, if you are wondering the importance of these programming paradigms, these outlined capabilities and properties show the extent in which neural networks are useful.

- Adaptability

One of the notable features of a neural network is the ability to adapt its synaptic weight to the environment. Exposure of a neural network to a different setting does not disrupt its functionality; instead, it can be retrained to accommodate any changes within its operating environment. The adaptive capability makes the neural networks to perform exemplary in signal processing, control functions, and classification of patterns. The adaptability of this system results in a robust performance.

- Nonlinearity

A neural network is mostly non-linear because the interconnections involve non-linear neurons. Nonlinearity enhances the neural networks' robustness in capacity recognition during the process of augmenting data. Additionally, the nonlinearity plays a central role in generating input signals such as speech signal.

- Fault Tolerance

Neural networks have an inherent nature to tolerate faults. In simple terms, the network has a robust computation that is incapable of degradation when the operating conditions are adverse. In a case where there is damage to the connecting links or the actual neurons, the quality of the stored data becomes poor.

Nonetheless, the distribution nature of neural networks reduces network degradation unless the damage is highly extensive. As such, it is rare for a neural network to experience a catastrophic failure. It is crucial to train the neural network to be fault-tolerant in case of damage.

- Input and Output Mapping

In supervised learning, the neural networks modify their synaptic weights by using training examples. Each of these examples has exclusive input signals, with an equivalent desired response. The examples help the system to learn, leading to the construction of an input and output mapping.

- Uniformity in Design and Analysis

One of the features that characterize neural networks is the universality of information processors. The aspect of uniformity is evident when neurons represent a common ingredient that relates to all the neural networks. The commonality further enables the sharing of learning algorithms and theories in neural networks applications. More importantly, modules can integrate seamlessly to build modular networks.

The properties of artificial neural networks make them advantageous and highly applicable in the real world. Programmers can choose the type of neural network with multiples capabilities.

Bayesian Networks

The growth of the Bayesian network is attributable to Thomas Bayes, who invented the Bayes rule in the 1700s. He came up with the law of probability that facilitates the update of changing probabilities. The concept of Bayesian Network in the 1980s was by Judea Pearl, who considered the differentiation of causal and evidential reasoning.

Bayesian networks have been gaining significant attention in different domains. Broadly, Bayesian Model refers to a framework that enables reasoning during uncertainty with the use of probabilities. It utilizes a probabilistic graphical language that promotes reasoning and knowledge representation. A BN has directed acrylic graph structure. The graph has different nodes corresponding to random variables. The edges are a representation of conditional dependencies. Unconnected nodes represent conditionally independent variables. Each of the nodes relates to a CP Table and provides specifications on the state of the nodes. Bayesian networks use principles from statistics, computer science, graph theory, and probability theory. The diagram below is an illustration of the Bayesian network as a graphical model.

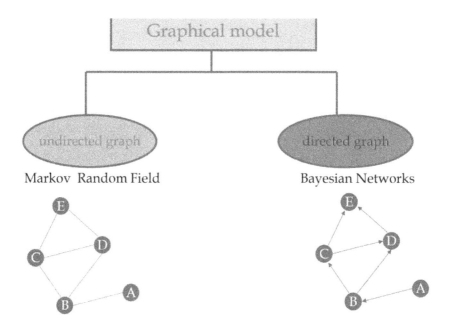

Besides the model's qualitative part encompassing the DAG, it is crucial to highlight the quantitative parameters of BN. The parameters build on the Markovian property in which the CPD within each of the nodes is solely dependent on the parents. A table represents the conditional probability of a discrete random variable. A CPT determines any joint distribution of variables. Bayesian networks are useful because they provide relevant knowledge in causal learning. They have probabilistic and causal semantics that facilitate a combination of prior data and knowledge. BN allows encoding dependency among variables.

Bayesian networks are in different types, and each of the categories addresses specific situations that might not be possible when using the model as a whole. The dynamic Bayesian network is a unique structure that models a temporal process. The DBNs provide indispensable representations because they go beyond the description of probabilistic relationships. The DBNs are in two parts; the prior BN and the transition BN. The first part is a general network, while the second part differs slightly because of the available structure. The latter has several arcs and nodes that are not present in the first network.

The causal interaction network is a distinct Bayesian network where the parents are independent. The noisy-OR model is one of the common types of causal interaction models. The decision networks, also known as influence diagrams, are special BNs that enhance decision making in uncertain situations.

Applications of Bayesian networks are diverse. Originally, BN was mostly applicable in medicine, which continues to be dominant today. However, the aspect of predictions has made

Bayesian network stand out in different fields. In forecasting, Bayesian networks make accurate predictions based on available knowledge. The HailFinder network is one of the BN applications that have been forecasting weather. In economics, the Bayesian network has been forecasting oil prices to determine market trends.

In medicine, BN plays several central roles. One of the most notable applications is the quick medical reference, which is a diagnosis system. The system considers the disease, background, and symptoms. With the numerous arcs and nodes within the system, developing algorithms to make inferences was inevitable. The Pathfinder project is another diagnostic system used in diagnosing the lymph-node disease. On the other hand, the MUNIN network has been useful in the diagnosis of neuromuscular conditions. The ALARM network developed in 1989 has been essential in monitoring patients receiving intensive care.

The Bayesian network is an easily implementable algorithm with a guaranteed accuracy of results in most cases. Its ability to take linear time makes it scalable to big datasets. One of the primary advantages of Naïve Bayes is that the algorithm doesn't need a large amount of training dataset to make an accurate estimation of the parameters. Additionally, the classifiers are faster than most of the other methods. The issue of zero probability in the Bayesian network is of concern to many users. When an attribute has zero conditional probability, the prediction is hardly valid. The use of a Laplacian estimator is necessary in such instances.

Support Vector Machine

Support Vector Machine is a recent development when compared with other models of machine learning. Vapnik, Guyon, and Bosser coined the term Support Vector Machine in 1992. SVM refers to a set of interrelated methods of supervised learning, mostly used for regression and classification. SVMs are in the category of linear classifiers. Support Vector Machine is a regression and classification prediction tool utilizing the theory of machine learning to enhance predictive accuracy. Initially, SVM was common in the NIPS community; today, it has become a critical part of machine learning research. The popularity of SVM results from the accuracy of outcomes when the input is in pixel maps. The figure below shows the classes defining support vectors.

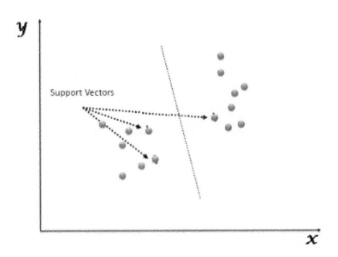

How does the SVM work? For non-professionals in the field, understanding SVM might seem complicated. You can follow a more straightforward approach to understand the concept. The first stage is the identification of hyper-planes, A, B, or C. The hyper-plane that you choose should have the ability to segregate classes. In the second scenario, you will need to increase the distances between the data points. With a high margin, the robustness of classification increases. Low margins lead to misclassification. In the third scenario, you already have the hyper-plane with the most upper margin. SVM considers the issue of classification errors and selects a hyper-plane that seems more accurate.

Support Vector Machine is applicable in several domains, including face and handwriting analysis for application based on regression and classification. The basis of SVM formulation is the principle of Structural Risk Minimization, which is more effective as compared to the conventional principle of Empirical Risk Minimization utilized by neural networks. SRM reduces the risk expected in upper bound, increasing the ability of a Support Vector Machine to generalize. The intended role of SVM was addressing classification problems; however, it is gaining popularity in solving regression problems.

The types of Support Vector Machines are classified based on their roles. The least-squares SVM is one of the versions developed by Vandewalle and Suykens. Its primary function is to recognize patterns and analyze data for regression analysis and classification. To find the solution when using this method, you have to solve several linear equations. The structured SVM is another version that enhances classifiers' training to promote labels with structured outputs. The Support Vector Clustering is a type of SVM mostly involved in cluster analysis. The process involves partitioning of data to group it into a meaningful form. In Support Vector Clustering, one maps the data points from the data space through the kernel function. Transductive SVM is a type of reasoning based on observed training and test cases. The method is applicable in supervised learning. One-class SVM, developed by Scholkopf is a type of SVM that helps in anomaly detection.

All the Support Vector Machines have their advantages and disadvantages. One of the pros is that SVM is significantly effective, especially in spaces with high dimensions. When there is a clear separation margin, the accuracy level of SVM is desirable. Besides, it produces quality results even when the samples are fewer than the dimensions. SVM is memory efficient following its use of support vectors within the decision function.

Conversely, SVM has the shortcomings that might make it less common as compared to other ML models. SVM underperforms in cases where the dataset is significant because of the high training time. In instances where there is overlapping of target classes, the performance is poor. When using SVM, you will have to use the fivefold cross-validation because the model does not give probability estimates. With the mentioned pros and cons, it is easier to work with SVM and other complementing approaches towards enhancing accuracy.

Model Optimization

One of the recent developments in the field of computer science is the interplay between machine learning and optimization. The different formulations in optimization have been essential in the design of algorithms that extract relevant knowledge from large data volumes. Machine learning is increasingly generating new ideas on optimization. The approaches are prominent because of their attractive theoretical properties and broad applicability. Optimization models are in two categories; constrained and unconstrained. The strategies in unconstrained optimization include Gradient descent, Stochastic Gradient Descent, and Newton's method.

Gradient Descent is a popular algorithm that trains several models of machine learning. This approach is one of the iterative models that analyze biases and weights. Gradient Descent minimizes the cost function. The process is sequential, with the first step being the random initialization of weights (W). The second step is the calculation of the gradients, which is through a partial differentiation $G = \partial J(W)/\partial W$. G is the gradient's value, which depends mostly on current values, the input, and cost function. The next step involves updating the weight, in which the amount should be proportional to the gradient. Repeat the process until you reach the cost stability of $J(W)$.

Stochastic is one of the common types of optimization's Gradient Descent. Stochastic refers to a process or a system linked to a random probability. This approach involves a random selection of samples for each of the iteration. While using the entire dataset can enable one to get absolute minima, batches are highly effective when the dataset is huge.

The Newton method of optimization, also referred to as Newton-Raphson utilizes two derivatives. The first step involves having a guess closely related to the root. The next step is the use of calculus for approximation and in finality, uses the elementary algebra for x-intercept computation. The method has several limitations that make it difficult to use. One, it is hard to calculate a function's derivative. Besides the high cost of evaluating an analytical expression, getting the derivative is not easy. The method may fail to converge to the root because of unmet assumptions. Another issue is poor initial estimation, which leads to the algorithm's non-convergence. Regardless of the flaws, optimization algorithms remain ideal because they reduce the error function resulting from the internal parameters of a model.

Further research on machine learning is vital to deconstruct the existing myth on this vast growing technology. Within the next few years, machine learning will be a central part of our daily activities. Learning the models and applications of this field will give you an edge especially in business.

Chapter 4: Probabilistic Models

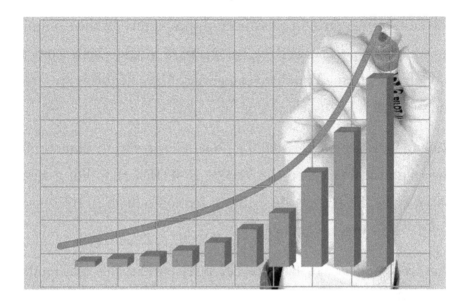

Machine learning algorithms can be classified in many ways. This chapter looks at the models briefly before discussing the probabilistic models of machine learning in-depth. The mode of explanation reflects the comparative analysis approach. While the book strives to give an understanding of the probabilistic models, it essential to note that the other models are equally worth a mention in this chapter.

Logical models

There are two categories of logical models. The types are tree models and rule models. The two groups make use of logical functions to split the instance spaces, creating classes. A rational function can be said to be one that gives a different value such a yes or no result.

In a logical expression, once the data has been categorized, it is then divided into homogeneous categories for the problem to be solved. For instance, in classification problems, all the example in a given type are said to belong to a single class. Logical models are grouped into two categories. The categories are; tree models and rule models.

Rule models are comprised of a pool of suggestions. Sometimes the rule model is called the WHAT IF-THEN rule. For a tree-based rule, the IF part describes a section and the THEN part defines how the section behaves.

The tree models can be considered as part of the rule model where the IF and THEN segments are structured in the form of a tree. Both the tree model and the rule model works in the same way as supervised learning. The approach taken by the two models can be summarized as follows.

The first method is finding the concept of the rule (its body) that deals with adequately standardized sets then find a label that represents the concept. The second method is targeting a specific study class and then determining the rules that cover the features in that class.

Geometric models

In the previous section on logical models, we have seen that rational expressions are used to divide the instance space. In this section, we will take into account designs that explain comparisons by making an allowance for the geometry of the instance space. Geometric models represent features in two or three dimensions (the x and y-axis or the x, y, and z-axis). Geometric models have both linear and distance-based models. In linear models, the features are represented in direct arrangements of the inputs in the element. In the range-based model, functions are described based on the difference of distance between two points within the task. The charts below represent the two model used in the geometric representation of functions.

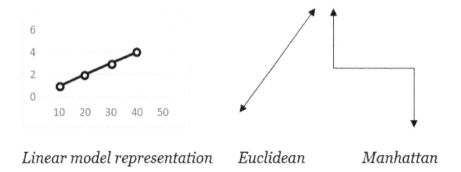

Linear model representation   *Euclidean*   *Manhattan*

Probabilistic models

In understanding probabilistic models, I will try to elaborate on the concept by breaking it down. The first section will explain the term probabilistic while the second section will go straight in detailing the models.

A probabilistic technique or model is based on the theory of uncertainty (probability) or the notion that chance can play a role in forecasting future events. The opposite of this model is deterministic, which entails the accurate determination of events through facts and not chance.

Probabilistic models integraterandom variables and prospect arrangement into the model of an incident or an occurrence. The probabilistic model offerslikelihooddissemination as a result. On the other hand, deterministic models that give a single solution to a given problem. The two models work by because a situation may not present all the factors needed to analyze it. Therefore, there is always a provision for random selection.For example, we can explain the situation using a life insurance policy. The policy takes into account the fact we will die. What is unknown is the date and the circumstances of death.

Probabilistic models can also be partly deterministic or entirely random. Random values from standarddispersal, binomial dissemination and Bernoulli distribution create the basis for probabilistic designs.

Probabilistic Method

The probabilistic methods are ways to verify the presence of structures with definite characteristics in groupings. The concept entails the creation of probability space, proving that the elements within the area have the qualities studied. Probabilistic methods are applied in various fields such as statistics, computer science, and quantum physics.

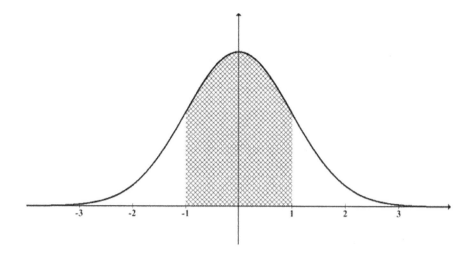

A standard distribution curve, (also called a bell curve) is one of the elements that create a probabilistic model

Probabilistic models can be subdivided into two units, graphical models and stochastic models.

Graphical models

In general, probabilistic graphical models utilize representation based on graphs as the groundwork for encrypting a dispersal over a multi-dimensional space. The models also use diagrams, which are condensed illustration of variables found in the limited distribution. There are two known types of graphs used probabilistic models. The two methods are Bayesian networks and Markov random fields. The techniques incorporate the functionalities of factorization and unconventionality. However, they are different in the way they prompt factorization and translatefairness.

Bayesian Networks

The Bayesian networks are a category of probabilistic graphical replicas, which are sometimes used to construct a different model from data or expert opinions. Bayesian networks can be used for many tasks. In machine learning, the Bayesian networks are used for estimation, detection of a fault in a set of data, diagnostic reasons, computerized intuition, and reasoning, calculating time series, and making decisions that fall under undefined circumstances. The table below is a representation of the aptitudes in four significant analytical terms. The terms are Graphic analytics, Problem-solving analytics, projecting analytics, and Dogmatic analytics.

Graphic analytics	Problem-solving analytics	Projecting analytics	Dogmatic analytic
Computerized insight	Information value	Supervised or unsupervised	Decision automation
Large patterns	Reasoning	Anomaly detection	Decision making based on cost
Anomalous patterns	Troubleshooting	Time series	Decision support
multivariate	Anomaly detection	Latent variations	Decision making under uncertainty

The representations are sometimes called the Bayes nets, Belief Networks, or Causal networks.

Characteristics of Bayesian networks

Probabilistic: Bayesian networks are predictive. The Bayesian networks are structured from distributions that are based on likelihood/chance. The Bayesian networks also follow the rule of probability to make forecast and detect faults for reasoning and problem solving, making decisions under uncertain conditions, and calculating time series.

Graphical: as shown in the image below, Bayesian networks are represented in graphical forms. The best way of learning the Bayesian network is through graphical representation. However, this method is optional.

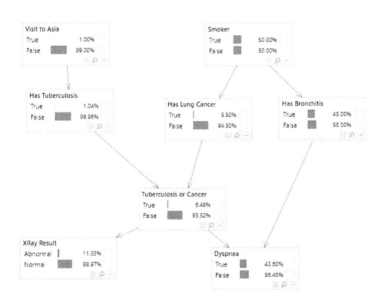

A simple Bayesian network, (called the Asia network)

A Bayesian network can be represented by a graph with nodes consisting of directed links in between them.

Nodes: in a Bayesian network, the node represents a known variable; for example, the age of a person. The feature can either be distinct, for instance, the size of a building (large or small) or continuous, for example, the age of a person.

In a Bayes server, the nodes consist of numerous parameters. Nodes that include multiple parameters (more than one setting) are called multi-variable nodes. The nodes and links infuse to create the structure of the Bayesian network. This infusion is called the structural specification. Bayes structures are built to support both distinct and continuous parameters.

Distinct variables: a discrete or separate variable is a parameter that contains a jointly exclusive state, for instance, complexity (light or dark)

Continuous variable: a continuous variable is one that can depend on each other. A Bayes server is built to sustain constant parameters with the Conditional Linear Gaussian distributions (CLG). CGL process means that the sparsity of the feature in a continuous form is in such a way that the variables rely on each other (hence considered to be multivariate). Additionally, constant variables can also rely on one or more distinct variables.

The conditional linear Gaussian distribution can mould a multifaceted non-linear and hierarchical relationship in a set of data. This ability comes in play even though Gaussians are perceived to be limiting. The Bayes servers are also capable of sustaining latent variables that can mould concealed relationships of data. The ability to model such a structure is called Programmed feature extraction, which is comparable to hidden layers in an artificial neural network.

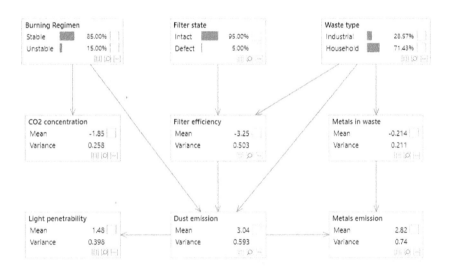

Links: links are add-ins that are infused between nodes to show the effect of a node on the other node. In some cases, a node may be connected by other nodes, which means that a link may not be available. In such a circumstance, the node is not considered independent. However, the node can become independent or dependent on the others as long as there is visible evidence of its relationship with other nodes. Information in a Bayesian structure can flow in either direction even though the links within the structure are directed. The flow, however, follows strict rules not discussed in this book.

Structural learning: a Bayes network consists of a necessary learning algorithm within the Bayes server. The first learning algorithm is capable of robotically determining the needed links from a given set of data. It is worth noting that there are various methods of solving different problems within the scope of a Bayes network. For this reason, structural learning may not be required.

Feature selection: a Bayes server is configured in a way that supports feature selection. The feature selection algorithm helps determine the variables that are most likely to have an impact on others. This method is advantageous in studying the structure of a specific model. Using latent variables is another method that can prove convenient in automatic extraction of features as part of the larger model.

Directed acyclic graphs (DAG): A simple Bayesian network is producing a type of chart known as the directed acyclic graph, abbreviated as DAG. A directed acyclic graph is a type of diagram with no directed cycles but contains directed links.

Directed cycles: A directed period in a Bayesian represented graph is a track beginning and ending at the same node. In this type of chart, the track taken can only lead through the direction of links.

Other categories of probabilistic graphical models

Other probabilistic models include;

Tree-augmented classifier or the TAN model

Naive Bayes classifiers

Naive Bayes classifiers are centred on the Bayes' hypothesis. The theory of classification by Bayes assumes independence among crucial variables in a set of data. Shortly put, the Naïve Bayes classification mechanism believes that a particular aspect in a class of data is not related to the next level. The application of the Naïve Bayes classifiers is suitable in the classification of widespread sets of data.

Decision Tree Classifiers

The decision tree prototype makes a classification in the structure of a tree. The decision tree is built to spread and break down data into smaller division, taking the form of branches of the tree. The result is, therefore, in the way of decision bulges and leaf bulges. A decision bulge, say the root grows to produce more than one branch. The leaf bulge signifies a classified class (in this case a decision). The first class/decision is the tree corresponding to the best predictive value (root). The decision tree classifiers can solve arithmetical and clear-cut problems.

Deep Deterministic Policy Gradient

The DDPG is a type of reinforcement learning that banks on the actor vs critic model. The actor component is applied to adjust the feature θ for the program function. In essence, for each state, the algorithm has to decide the best course of action to take. The algorithm also borrows a leaf from deep Q-learning, especially on the concepts of the separate target network and capability reiteration. Occasionally, the system performs a survey for the actions. However, this is neutralized by the addition of noise to the functionality space.

Types of graphs

Factor graph

This is an undirected split graph which joins variables and metrics. Each factor is a representation of a specific function over the variable it is linked to. This type of graph is useful in understanding and instigating belief transmission.

Chain graph

A chain is a type that is both directed and undirected. However, the figure lacks a directed cycle. Good examples of chain graphs include directed acyclic graphs and undirected graphs. These graphs can provide ways of joining and simplifyingtheBayesian and Markov networks.

Ancestral graph

An ancestral graph is one with further extensions consisting of undirected, a bi-directed, and directed ends.

Random Field Techniques

Markov Decision Processes

MDP is an algorithm of reinforcement learning. The algorithm consists of real value reward functions, model sets, a collection of probable actions, a pool of likely world states, and a policy. For effectiveness, the Markov Decision Processes uses an open framing method to study the relationship of variables. The component here selects an action that corresponds to the natural effects within the environment. The two steps are then made to correlate to present new situations to the element

A Markov random field (also called the Markov network), is a model over a graph that is not directed. In Markov Network, a graphical prototype with numerousrecurrent sub-divisions can be exemplified with plate representation.

Stochastic Models

A stochastic model is a type of probabilistic model that exemplifies condition where uncertainty is present. In simple words, it is a model for processes that possess unpredictability. In the real world, improbability forms part of our daily life. For this reason, a stochastic model can represent everything. The reverse of this model is a deterministic model, which forecastsresults with 100% conclusion. As opposed to deterministic models, stochastic models gives a different outcome every time the model is run.

All stochastic models have the following standard features.

1. All models reflect all the given features of the studied element.

2. Chances are allocated to measures within the model.

3. The changes within the model can be utilized to predict or give further information about the element of study.

Chapter 5: Soft Computing

As the term suggests, soft computing is the concept of figuring out problems in a smooth way. The methods involved in soft computing tend to work out problems the way human beings would. Lofti Zadeh first visualized the idea. Zadeh pioneered the mathematical concept of Fuzzy sets. The Fuzzy sets have enabled developments in various fields of computation. Such areas include fuzzy graph theory, fuzzy control system etc. In his argument, he observed that people think softly as opposed to computers which are hard thinkers. The difference in the concept can be drawn from the terms that people used as opposed to what machines use.

Expression of people	Computers expressions
Quantitative terms like most, some, etc.	Precise terms like 3, 499, etc.
General terms like warm, cold, etc.	Exact terms like 100 degrees Celsius

In general comparison, human beings learn, find patterns, adapt to changes in the environment and are very unpredictable. On the other hand, machines learn to be precise, use metrics, are fragile to changes,

From the above inclination, we can understand soft computing as developing the model that is not so much organized or programmed to fit one course. The computers must be flexible. These are neural models which are highly bendable. There is, however, no single method that allows computers to compute like humans. For this reason, soft computing revolves around the use of a collection of ways that bend towards achieving flexibility.Machine learning is one of the main components that underline the concept of soft computing.

Soft computing has continued to be a necessary scope of study in computer science and IT since the 90s. The traditional approaches of computation could replicate andaccuratelyexploresimple patterns alone. More complex problems in fields such as biology and mathematics became challenging to solve using the conventional methods of analysis.

For these purposes, soft computing was introduced to solve the grey areas of imprecision, improbability, fractional truth, and estimations to make computability possible and at a lower cost. In this sense, soft computing forms the basis of a substantial amount of machine learning methods. New inventions and development s tend to reflect evolutionary and cloud intelligence that is based on algorithms that are inspired by biological processes, such as artificial neural networks.

In general terms, soft computing methods bear a resemblance to biological procedures. The arrangements are not inclined to formal logic techniques and do not depend heavily on computer-supported arithmetical analysis.

Contrary to hard computing formats that go all-out for exactitude and precision, soft computing techniques make use of certainforbearance of vagueness, fractional truth, and improbabilityfor a meticuloushitch. Another generaldistinctioncan be drawn from the significance of roles played in the two methods.

Components of Soft Computing

There are several components of soft computing. The major ones include:

1. Machine learning (Neural networks, which encompass Perceptron and support vector machines)

2. Fuzzy logic

3. Evolutionary computation

4. Metaheuristic and cloud Intelligence

5. Probabilistic ideas(including the Bayesian network)

Of all the components, this book will dwell mostly on the machine learning front. The direction taken by this book is generally based on the scope and context of the book. Other components will be discussed in the next issue. The machine learning component of soft computing primarily focuses on ANN and SVM. As discussed in the opening chapters of the book, the two will be addressed in a slightly different angle.

Support vector machines in soft computing

At this point in learning, I suppose the reader is familiar with both linear regression and logistic regression algorithms. The knowledge in the areas is very vital in understanding SVMs. The support vector machine is a simple algorithm recommended for anyone wishing to dive in the field of machine learning. Machinelearning experts mostly use the SVM model due to its ability to give results with striking accuracy will less calculation power. Support vector machine, otherwise abbreviated as SVM can be applied in both classification and regression tasks. However, SVM is broadly used for classification purposes.

Understanding a support vector machine in soft computing

The support vector machine is usually purposed to find a hyperplane in an N-Dimension space. This statement can be summarized in a formulation where N is the number of parameters that categorize the data points.

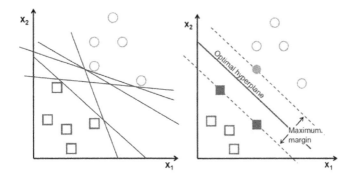

Probable hyperplanes

Various possible hyperplanes can be used to sort out the two classes of data points. The end goal is finding the plane with the highest margin; in essence, the thoroughgoing distance between the two data points in the classes. Getting the best out of the margin distance would allow for future reinforcement such that the following data points are easy to classify.

Relationship between hyperplanes and support vectors

A hyperplane in $\mathbb{R}^2$ is a line

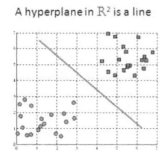

A hyperplane in $\mathbb{R}^3$ is a plane

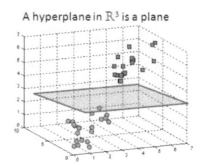

Two-dimensional and three-dimensional hyperplanes

Hyperplanes can be defined as the decision borders that are used in classifying the data points. The data points that stray on either side of the hyperplane can be classified in different classes. The dimension quality of the hyperplane is exclusively reliant on the number of parameters/metrics within the set of data. If there are only two features in the input data, then the hyperplane will assume a line dividing the features. If the number of elements in the input data is three, then the hyperplane will consider a two-dimensional plane. Functionality beyond three in the input data become hard to solve using the hyperplane.

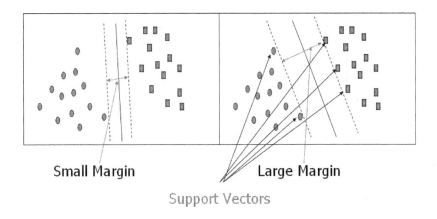

Small Margin   Large Margin

Support Vectors

Support Vectors

Support vectors are data points that stray closer to the hyperplane (as shown in the image above). The support vector impacts the location and the alignment of the hyperplane. The use the support vectors can maximize the margin of the classifier. When the support vectors are deleted, the position of the hyperplane changes. In general, the points within the hyperplane are useful in structuring a support vector machine.

The awareness of the large margin

In logistic regression, the output value of the linear function is taken and compressed within the range of 0-1 by the use of the sigmoid function. If the compressed amount is more significant than a threshold value of 0.5, it is assigned a mark (1). If the value is smaller than the threshold value, it is assigned the score (0).

In support vector machines, the output value of the linear function is taken, and if that output is more significant than 1, the cost is identified with a single class. In cases where the output value is lesser than 1, the value is determined with another type. Since the threshold values are changed to 1 and -1 (value below 1) in support vector machine, the reinforcement range of benefits (-1 and 1) that performs as the margin is obtained.

Neural networks as a component of soft computing

Sometimes referred to as artificial neural networks, these models have been defined in broad context by major players in the field. Deriving from Dr Robert Hecht-Nielsen, I want my readers to digest this component as;

A model of computation that is made of modest, largely intersected features that extract usefulness from data through their active reaction to outward inputs.

Artificial neural networks are devices (software devices, i.e., algorithms or hardware) that process information and are roughly molded to resemble the components of the human brain, but on lower levels. More extensive neural networks consist of many units that process data. In contrast, the human brain is made up billions of neurons that correspond with a rise in the extent of general relations and evolving conduct.

The Basics of Neural Networks in soft computing

Artificial neural networks are characteristically grouped in layers. The layers are completed with numerous intersected nodes containing specific performance feature. Different designs are infused I the layers by the use of an input layer. The input layer interconnects to other layers within the network. The layers in the network perform the actual processing through a system of subjective associates. The segments that are connected with the input layer link with the output layer.

Many artificial neural networks have different forms of training rules which refine the connections within the layers in the system, per the input data design. As a child learns to identify objects in the environment by seeing and interacting with the item, so does neural network learn?

This book will explore the delta rule learning method as used by neural networks. Note that the neural networks can use other rules. In most cases, the delta rule is applied by collective classes of ANN known as the 'backpropagation neural networks.' Backpropagation is an acronym for the backward transmission of fault.

Similar to other types of backpropagation, the delta rule training method is a supervised process. The process occurs in epochs (the cycle of presenting new data input in the network) by a forward flowing functional output. The flow of the production corresponds with the backward propagation of error. The neural network predicts the type of data each time it is infused in the network. The prediction is followed by the interpretation of the deviation of the answer given from the actual answer. The system then makes correct adjustments. It is worth noting that every layer connected to the input layer consist of a sigmoidal functional unit, which separates the activities of the network hence creating stability.

Backpropagation achieves an inclined pedigree within the solution's vector space concerning a 'universal minimum' end to end with the vector of the error function. The universal minimum is the hypothetical explanation with the least probable fault. The error surface can be looked at as a hyper-paraboloid. It is, however, even as illustrated in most graphical representations. For most problems, the answer is always contained in an irregular answer space. The irregularity of the area makes the network to settle on the local minimum, which may not be the most suitable solution.

How the delta rule finds the correct answer

The nature of the error space is sometimes hard to establish before the study. For this reason, the neural network analysis, in most cases, require several trials to produce the most suitable answer. Most learning rules have arithmetic terms as extensions to help in controlling the beta-coefficient and the momentum of the process of learning. The beta-coefficient is always the rate of merging between the real answer and the universal minimum. The Momentum of the learning process supports the network to overcome snags and settle for a value that is the global minimum of the value closet to it.

The neural network is often used as a tool to analyze other sets of data once the network if fully trained. At this level, the user may not require to specify any testing procedures. Instead, the user lets the system to perform in a headfirst propagation approach alone. New data inputs are infused in the responsive design. The data is then filtered into the plan and are sort out by the mid-layers in a manner that resembles the training process. Retention of the input data happens at this point while no backpropagation happens. The resultant output (in a headfirst propagation) becomes the forecast model for the data. The output data can be used for auxiliary breakdown and clarification.

In some instances, the neural network gets trained to answer back to a single type of data input accurately. This situation is considered as an over-training of the neural network. The process works more like a routine memorization process. Such circumstance requires the learning process of the system to cut shot and is therefore referred to as a grand-mothered network within the neural network redundancy. The application of this method is, however, not common in real life.

As a component of soft computing, neural networks can be broken down to focus on perceptron.

What is a Perceptron?

A perceptron canbe defined as a simple unit of a neural network. The group is capable of doing the following.

1. Taking arithmetical values along with its weight as input in the centre.

2. Calculating the weighted sum and gives a return of 1 if the summation is positive.

A perceptron can also be considered a model for computation that draws a boundary (a line in two-dimensional cases) to isolate two classes in a given space.

Initially, the weights and the bias which represents the classification hyperplane is usually unknown. In this case, random weights and partiality are allocated to the model.The random assignment leads to misclassification of points.

The Perceptron trick

The objective of the perception trick is decreasing the amount of misclassified points. The reduction can be made by sliding the line over the space. In other words, it is altering the expression of the hyperplane. For all the wrongly categorized points, we adjust the weights and bias to move the hyperplane closer to the points that are improperly classified. After some time, the algorithm will rectify the problem to classify the points correctly.

Chapter 6: Data Mining

Data mining is a trendy field in machine technology. The concept was first generated in the 90s. The idea of data mining has been, in broad perspective, referred to as big data or data science. The definition of this concept varies depending on the application and scope. In this book, I will look at data mining as the process of extracting raw sets of data for analysis and discovery of more knowledge about the collection.

Thanks to the advancement in computer networks, data can now be stored effectively and cheaply. Additionally, the transfer of data has been enhanced due to the availability of electronic sources. These reasons and many more have enabled the spread of data mining techniques. Many organizations are thereby able to store massive amounts of data in databases without the fear of losing sensitive information.

The ability to store vast amounts of data in databases is excellent. However, it is also essential to know how to analyze and interpret the sets of data at your disposal. Possessing larges sets of data that we cannot explain and draw meaningful information from is as good as having no data at all. That brings the question on how to analyze data stored in various databases. Traditional methods of analyzing data included the manual hand analysis process. However, conventional methods have proved to be time-consuming, tedious, and the result may not reflect accurate outcomes. The traditional ways missed critical information in datasets making the analysis processes a miss.

Additionally, the emergence of massive sets of data have made conventional techniques irrelevant and unrealistic. To mitigate the problems, automated methods have been designed to help sort data and extract useful information, trends and patterns that may be desirable. The field is where data mining methods and techniques come in handy.

In clear terms, data mining processes aim at explaining the outcome of an event, forecasting future results, and helping in understanding complex data. The science of data mining have been used to describe phenomena such as why a ship sank or plane crushed. In aeroplanes, data mining is done through black boxes fit with datasets and information about every flight. This way, it easy to tell the circumstances that led to a crush. As opposed to other machine learning methods of predicting outcomes, data mining techniques are used to foretell the possible outcome based on facts and not instinct.

The process for analyzing data

For an efficient means of data mining, there must be an observance of seven steps called the knowledge discovery in databases. The seven stages of knowledge discovery in databases are illustrated below.

Data cleaning. This is the first step in analyzing data. In this phase, data is cleaned to remove noise and other variations that may hamper proper analysis.

Data integration. The second step following data cleaning is data integration. This process involving linking, infusing and incorporating data from various sources to prepare the data that is to be analyzed. For instance, if the information is stored in different databases, integration is done to put the data together in one database.

Data selection. After data is put together in a single file, the relevant set is chosen for analysis. This is a process called data selection.

Data transformation. Having done all the procedures above, the data is now ready to be converted into a fitting format. The conversion is done to make analysis easy. For instance, some techniques of mining data may require that all arithmetic values be standardized.

Data mining. This step involves the application of data mining algorithms to analyze the data and extract meaningful patterns and information from the analyzed sets of data.

Assessment of the extracted patterns and knowledge. This step in data mining involves the study and evaluation of the derived patterns and information from the analyzed data. The review of results can be done in subjective or objective terms.

Visualization of data. The last step in the data mining process is the conception of the extracted information from the analyzed data. This step is when we try to understand the outcome.

It is essential to know that the steps above may vary depending on the technique and the algorithms used. For instance, some algorithms of data mining may perform the steps concurrently or continuously.

Application of data mining in related fields

Several data mining algorithms can be used in the various sectors and domains where data analysis is vital. Some of these applications are listed below.

1. Detection of fraud

2. Prediction of stock market valuations

3. Analyzing the purchasing patterns of clients

In a broad sense, the techniques of data mining are chosen based on the following metrics.

1. The type of data to be analyzed

2. Theform in which the information extracted from datasets is required.

3. The application of extracted knowledge (how the information is used).

Relationship between data mining and other research areas

Data mining is an inter-categorical field of study that overlaps and corresponds to different segments such as machine learning, computer science, soft computing, etc. The relationship between data mining and these fields overlay the fundamental notion of supplementing artificial intelligence.

This notion holds that each subsect and area in artificial intelligence complement each other and work both dependently and independently.

Data mining and statistics

There are striking differences between data mining and statistics. However, the two fields of research have many components and concepts in common.

In the past, descriptive statistics concentrated on labelling data using metrics, while inferential statistics put more weight on theoryanalysis to draw noteworthyinference from the data or generateprototypes. On the contrary, data mining techniques are more concerned about the outcome of the study as opposed toarithmeticalimplication. Many methods of data mining do not focus on the arithmetic test or connotation, as long as given metrics likeviability and precisionare met to the maximum. Additionally, data mining is usually concentrated on automated analysis of datasets, and in most cases by machinery that can scale to a massive amount of data. The proximity in scope is realized by mathematicians, who sometimes refer to data mining in statistics as "statistical learning."

Main data mining software

To successfully perform the process of data mining, there are some software and algorithmic computer program available. The software varies in model and use. Some software is all-purposeimplements that offer algorithms of different kinds.

Other software is more specified. It is important to note that some software is developed for commercial purposes, while others are free to access and configure (open-source). The various software can perform data mining onseveral data types.

Data mining software and algorithms are specifically developed to be used on different types of data. Below, I offer a summary of the countless examples of data generallybumped into, and which can be analyzed using the methods of data mining.

Relational databases: relational databases are the classic type of database that is mostly found in institutions and firms. In this form, data is categorically structured in tables. Conventional methods, like SQL, are used to query the database when trying to find faster information in the database. However, data mining enables the finding of sophisticated patterns within the database.

Customer transaction databases: another commonly used type of database is the customer transaction database. This type is mostly used in retail stores. The database is made up of all dealings made by the clients. The study of this database is essential in understanding the patterns of purchase and sales. It allows the retailers to understand the changes in the market, thus helping in planning sales and marketing strategy.

Temporal data: Another prevalent form of data is temporal data. The mundane type considers the time dimension in the data. Here, arrangements are created in many realms such as a sequence of items purchased by a customer, a chain of part of the population that is vegan, etc. The temporal data is further divided into time series. The series is a systematic list of arithmetic values like the price of shares in the stock market.

Spatial data: another set of data that can be easily analyzed is spatial data. This type of data consists of aggregate information like environmental data, forestry data, and data about substructures such as railway lines and air distribution channels.

Spatio-temporal data: this is a type of data that has both characteristics of spatial and temporal data. For instance, the data can be about climatic conditions, the movement of the wilder beast in crowds, etc.

Text data: the text type of data has become a widely studied area in data mining. The utilization spreads even though text data is mostly amorphous. Text documents are mostly disorganized and lack a definite form. Examples of text data are in feeling analysis and composition acknowledgement (predicting the author of a given text).

Web data: this a type of data that originates from websites. The data is mainly sets of a document, e.g. journals from the web with attached links. The sets are bound to form a graph. Some specific examples of data mining activities in the internet include predicting the possible next page in the website, grouping the webpages according to subjects automatically, and evaluating the time taken on every webpage.

Graph data:graphs is also another type of database. Charts are found in social networks (for instance, the list of Facebook friends) and chemistry (for example a graph of biochemical molecules and atoms).

Assorted data. Different or miscellaneous type of data is a collection of many kinds of data. The classes are linked and can be sorted into a specific arrangement.

Data streams: A data stream is said to be a continuous and high-speed torrent of data that is theoretically boundless. For instance, the data stream can be ecological data, data from video cameras, or digital television data). The limitation of this type of data is that it cannot be adequately stored in the computer. Therefore, the data should be evaluated regularly using suitable methods of data mining. Everyday data mining tasks in stream data are usually the detection of variations and tendencies.

Patterns found in data

As previously deliberated, the objective of data mining is to minedesirable patterns of information from data. The leading types of designs that can be extracted from data are as follows (take note that this list is not the finished product):

Clusters

Algorithms used I clustering are always applied in a situation where the sets of data are supposed to be sort in groups of similar instances (clusters). The main aim of these algorithms is condensing data to make it easy to understand and make an inference. Clustering modus operandi likes K-Means can be utilized to robotically group student showing similar performance.

Classification models

The algorithms used for classification tasks are purposed to extract models, which can be used to group objects and new instances into classes. For example, classification algorithms such as Naive Bayes, decision trees, and the neural networks can be used to create designs capable of predicting the trends in customer behaviours or the possibility of individual students to pass an examination. These models can also be hauled out to executea forecast about the future.

Patterns and associations

Some methods are designed to study the relationship between data and frequently occurring patterns.For instance, the frequency of an itemset can be analyzed, using data mining algorithms, to determine the most purchased items in particular retail outlets. Additional types of patterns are temporal patterns, progressive rules, irregular patterns, and recurrent subgraphs.

Anomaly detection

The AD is a method of machine learning that seeks to detect glitches and variances within a given set of data.

Simple Statistical Methods

The simplest way to detect anomalies within a set is to ensign the data points that strays from the mutual arithmetical properties of the distribution of the class of data. The features may take in the mean, median, mode, or quantiles. In simple terms the most variable data is one with the highest deviation from the central distribution unit, say the mean.

Anomaly detection approaches based on machine learning

There are a host of machine learning-based methods of anomaly detection. A brief overview of these methods is given below.

Density-Based Anomaly Detection

This technique is based on the concept of the K-nearest neighbour algorithm. In this process, an underlying assumption that standard data points ensue around a compressed neighbourhood and deviations are far away is made. The classes of data point that occur closest are calculated using a score. The score can be a Euclidian space or an analogous measure depending on whether the data is categorical or numerical. This approach can further be classified into two;

1. K-Nearest Neighbor algorithm: this is a simple, non-feature based learning procedure used to categorize data based on matches in distance metrics.

2. Local outlier factor: this approach is also called the relative density tactic. The method is entirely based on the reachability distance metric.

Clustering-Based Anomaly Detection

As discussed earlier in this book, clustering is a fundamental concept in the domain of unsupervised learning. In the clustering-based approach of anomaly detection, the assumption that similar data points tend to fall in the same classes/clusters (as determined by the distance from the core of the class) is made. The most used algorithm in this approach is the K—Means. The K-Means creates data points with similar "k" function in a cluster. Any data that finds itself out of the group is perceived to be irregular.

Support Vector Machine-Based Anomaly Detection

Another instrumental technique to detect an anomaly is by the use of the support vector machine. The support vector machine is typically associated with supervised earning. However, some add-ins can be used to detect irregularities in an unsupervised model. For the training set of data, the algorithm studies a soft boundary to group the standard data. On the other hand, the machine fine-tunes itself to recognize the irregularities that stray out of the learned region in the testing phase. The output of an anomaly indicator can be a numeric scalar value for clarifying on particular domain onsets or textual markers depending on the use.

Association rules

Association Rules is a very critical theory of machine learning. The concept is widely used in the market product pool analysis. For instance, in a shopping mall, you will find that utensils are placed on the same shelf, and all electronics are arranged in a similar rack. This type of product arrangement is meant to help the customers locate what they want in the shortest time possible. The layout is also usually appealing, which may remind a customer of the relevant kinds of stuff they might be fascinated with purchasing. The method thus allows the outlets cross-sell in the process.

Association rules make it possible to unearth the relationships between objects within a massive set of data. It is important to note that:-

Association rules do not mine the inclinations of an individual. However, the law learns the relationship between the items in different purchase records. This essential trait differentiates association rules from the collaborative filtering.

In association rules, the IDs of items purchased by customers are studied to identify the relationship between the elements. Details with similar traits are then considered separately in one group.

The diagram below can illustrate how an association rule looksooooo. The layout consists of original data and the resultant item. All the details are on a list. It is worth noting that inference here is co-occurrence and not connection. For any given rule, **item-set** is the list of all the items in the original set and the resultant set.

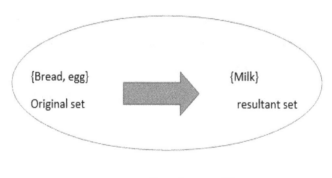

Item-set = {bread, egg, milk}

Numerous metrics can help in understanding the strength of the association between the two items.

1. Support

This metric helps by showing the frequency of the item-set in all purchase records. For instance, let us consider the first item-set to be {bread} and the second item-set to be {shoe polish}. In all purchase records, there will be more bread than shoe polish. For this reason, the first item-set will have more support than the second. The same treatment applies to item-sets that have more than one item. Arithmetically, support is the portion of the total purchase record in which the item-set occurs. Formulated as:-

Support ({A} => {B}) = (Total appearance of A and B in purchase record) / (Total number of purchases)

The value of support helps identify the rules to consider for additional scrutiny.

Confidence

This metric shows the probability of occurrence of the resultant set when the basket already has an original set. For instance, the metric will tend to explain the probability of milk appearing in a basket that already has bread and butter. For this case, we will find that {bread, butter} => {milk} have a higher confidence rule. Theoretically, confidence is the uncertain likelihood of occurrence of resultant given the original set.

Confidence ({A} => {B}) = (Purchase record with both A and B) / (Occurrence of A)

Lift

Lift controls the frequency (support) of the resultant in computing the uncertain likelihood of occurrence of item {B} given item {A}. Lift is considered a precise term for this process. Consider this example. Lift that {A} gives the possibility of the {B} occurring in the same basket. In other words, a lift is the increase in the likelihood of item {B} appearing in a basket when we know that the same basket contains item {A} over the likelihood of issue {B} appearing in a basket when we do not understand that the bucket has item {A}.

Lift ({A} => {B}) = (Transactions with A and B) (Transactions with A alone)/ (A section of transactions with B)

Trends and regularities

Data mining methods can be applied to study trends and uniformities in databases. Some applications of these patterns are forms that study the changes in the market valuation of shares and stock prices and make predictions on investments. Other applications are capable of findingsequences in the ways a system performs, and determine the order of events leading to system failure.

As mentioned previously, the aim of data mining is finding patterns in data and extracting useful information from the designs. Such occurrences like frequency and trends are essential components that underline the concept of data mining. As I have always said, it is crucial to find a balance that is suitable for yourself. The listed examples are only meant to give a brief overview of the concepts.

Chapter 7: Machine Learning Datasets

Numerous concepts underpin the general knowledge of machine learning. These components lay the foundation for understanding the field as well as making the processes a go.

In this chapter, my readers will get comprehensive information about the catalogue (standard terms) used to refer to data and datasets in machine learning. Additionally, I have availed a comprehensive analysis of the concepts and conditions that are used to build the literature on machine learning and datasets.

Data

As we have seen earlier, machine learning algorithms learn from examples. The most crucial element to note in this section is the input data and various terms used to describe these sets of data.

In this chapter, I would like to explain data in terms of rows and columns, similar to an excel spreadsheet. Data analyzed in this method reflects the traditional structure that is commonly used in machine learning. Unstructured data sets like images have not to be discussed here. The image below is a representation of sets of data used in machine learning algorithms.

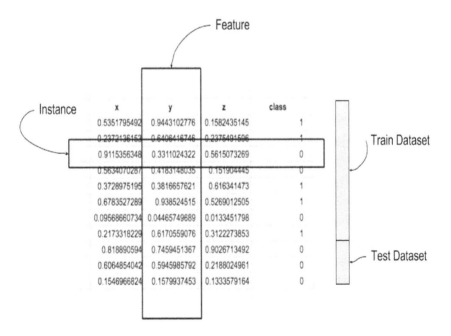

An image of data sets

Defining the terms

Instance: an instance is a single line (row) of data in a machine learning algorithm. A case is an inference from the realm.

Feature: a feature is a single column of data. An element is a constituent of observation and is also known as the attribute of a data instance. A function may also be called a metric or a parameter. Some of these metrics may be data inputs to an algorithm (the training data, also called the predictors) while others may be outputs (the parameters to be determined or predicted).

Data Type: metrics have different forms of data. Types of data may be actual or integer-valued. In other instances, the type of data may have a clear-cut or standard value. Additional classes may be in the form of strings, times, lengths, etc. When traditional machine learning techniques are used, the various types of data are reduced to real values.

Datasets: a dataset can be defined as a group of instances. Machine learning models usually require a few sets of data for variousfunctions.

Training Dataset: a set of data that is fed into the system to help guide the algorithm is called a training dataset. As the name suggests, they train the system.

Testing Dataset:

After training the machine learning model, it is essential to test their performance. The sets of data that are used to evaluate the accuracy of the algorithm are called testing datasets. Inother terms, they are called validation or evaluation datasets.

Learning

The focus here is based on machine learning. As seen, machine learning is all about training algorithms to perform tasks. In this perspective, we will take a look at some concept of learning

Induction: the algorithms in various models of machine learning are trained through a process known as induction or inductive learning. Induction is a process of deciding sweeping statements (generalization) from detailed information (training datasets).

Generalization: The notion is also called sweeping statements. The process is vital because the representationset by a machine learning algorithm is required to make forecasts. Such findings are based on specific data instances not present at the training phase.

Over-Learning: over-learning is described as the situation where an algorithm of machine learning observes the features in the training data too much but still fails to perform generalization. This situation is broughtabout by poor performance on data other than the training dataset. This instance is also known as over-fitting.

Under-Learning: under-learning is a situation whereby machine learning algorithms do not observe the training datasets to completion. The process may be caused by early termination f the training process — under-learning results in good generalization but poor performance on all data, not excluding the training dataset. The situation is also described as under-fitting.

Online Learning: online learning methods are instances when the data instance form a domain is used to update the system as the data become available.in online learning, robust processes that are not affected by noisy data are used. These methods can produce models that correspond to the current state domain.

Offline Learning: Offline learning is when a technique is produced on data that is pre-prepared to be used operationally on unlearned data. The process of training the system can be carefully tuned since the training dataset is known. After the preparation of the model, no further updates are made. This scenario may lower the performance in case there is a change in domain.

Supervised Learning: This is a method of machine learning that is used to generalize problems where a forecast is necessary. A "training process" compares predictions by the model to known answers and makes corrections in the model.

Unsupervised Learning: as discussed earlier, unsupervised learning is the process of generalization without any training data set being fed to the system. In this technique, naturally occurring structures are observed and utilized to interpret the relationship between the instances.

Modeling

A structure that is created by the process of machine learning is considered a model. The method of producing models is modeling.

Model Selection: the process of model selection can be described as the process in which configuration and training of a model of machine learning are done. In every given time, the system should present different models to modify, use, or discard. The choice of which algorithm to install in machine learning is also a part of model selection. For a given problem, the algorithms of machine learning will pick a model in which it operates.

Inductive Bias: a bias is an impartial input in a given model of machine learning. All machine learning models are biased to induce an error in the model. The failure caused is usually used to test the model or to act as a control set of data. Bias can be produced in a model during the configuration phase of the training phase. A machine learning algorithm can have a low or high preference depending on the input data. There are methods to remove high bias in algorithms.

Model Variance: variance the sensitivity of a model towards a training data set. Generally put, a variation is how a model responds to data input for training. A machine learning model can show high or low variance to training datasets. The best way to reduce the difference is by running the machine on a dataset over and over again. This process is done under different parameters and conditions. When variance has diminished the accuracy of the model is enhanced.

Bias-Variance Tradeoff: a model selection process can be regarded as a trade-off of the bias and the variance. The relationship between bias and variance is inverse proportionality. A model with low bias will possess high variation and will require longtime and continuous training to get a usable model. On the other hand, a model with high bias will maintain low variance, which makes it learn faster, but realizesadverse and limited performance.

Chapter 8: Machine Learning Vs Deep Learning

Both machine learning and deep learning are branches of artificial intelligence. The two areas have attracted a lot of focus over the years. This chapter offers the best place to understand the differences in these two areas in the most straightforward manner possible. In this chapter, I will explain the striking areas that differentiate the two models and help you point out the best way of incorporating the two.

Before I commence, I would wish to give you an overview of what the two terms mean (even though you are now familiar with the concept of machine learning).

Machine Learning

As explained earlier, machine learning is a subdivision of artificial intelligence. Machine learning involves the development of intelligent machines. These machines operate by the use of algorithms that are capable of mimicking human actions. In machine learning, the algorithms are built in a way that they performtasks without too much interference.

Deep Learning

Deep learning is also a subsect of artificial intelligence.In deep learning, the algorithms are built in the same way as those of machine learning. The difference is that in deep learning, there are many layers of algorithms. Each layer provides a different outcome of the input data. The layers are joined to form a network of algorithms. The systems are known as artificial neural networks (ANN). The artificial neural networks work in a way that imitates the functioning of the neural networks in the human brain.

To make the definitions simpler and point out the differences, we will take a look at an example.

Taking an example of images of boys and girls, we will go step by step in analyzing how machine learning ad deep learning would analyze the information.

Image an image of a boy and a girl. Now let us try to identify the images separately using machine learning algorithms and deep learning algorithms.

Solving the problem through Machine Learning

To enable categorization of images by machine learning algorithms, we have to feed the algorithm with the data (feature present) in both pictures. The feature, in this case, becomes the data input.

In line with the definition given above, the data must be structured. We have to mark the datasets with the features of both boys and girls. The input should be able to reflect the distinguishing features in both boys and girls.The data provided will aid the learning process of the algorithm. After that, the algorithm will be able to work based on the interpretation of the data input, thereby classifying more images of people into boys and girls.

Solving the same problem using Deep Learning

In addressing the same issue, deep learning will assume a different approach. The main hi in deep learning is that the networks do not require structured data (labelled) to classify images of people. The neural networks in deep learning interpret the images through layers of algorithms. Each layer in the interface defines a different feature on the image. The human brain works in the same way. The networks in deep learning will solve this problem by establishing question marks through an assortment of hierarchies of feature and other related components. The system determines the appropriate features that can classify the images following the processing of data in the algorithm layers.

Points to note

The best way to differentiate machine learning from deep learning is the mode in which information (input data) is presented to the systems. In machine learning, the algorithms mostly require labelled data (apart from unsupervised learning). On the other hand, deep learning relies on artificial neural networks to make simulations.

The algorithms of machine learning are deployed to "learn" how to perform specific tasks by interpreting marked data and then using it to process outcomes. However, the system needs to be trained again in case the findings do not meet the required standards. On the other hand, deep learning networks do not require a lot of training. The algorithmic layers in the neural networks pass data through hierarchies of diverse models. The models learn through the trial and error approach.

The quality of data impacts the quality of output. In other words, the systems try to work on the GIGO (garbage in garbage out) approach, which implies that the machine gives result according to the feed it receives. The quality of input is the governing factor in both systems.

Machine learning algorithms are not appropriate for solving problems that require a massive amount of data.

When to apply deep learning

Deep learning techniques are essential when the load of data required to solve a problem is massive. The artificial neural networks also come in handy when the issue at hand is very complicated. Lastly, you can use deep learning if you have the computational funds and operating cost to configure hardware and programs for training networks.

Chapter 9: Pros and Cons

This chapter focuses on the pros and cons of machine learning drawing analysis from both sides of the coin. The reader and potential users must take note of the bits that make machine learning a win and the feature that need review. This way, the balance is established to ensure proper incorporation of intelligent machines in our daily lives.

As shown, the advantages of machine learning do not rest solely on the ability to mine large sets of data and transform it into useful information. Many organizations have turned to machine learning to automate the functions of computer programs. This way, other methods of analyzing data are complemented

The first section will look at the benefits of machine learning that have not been mentioned in the above chapters. The advantages create massive openings that transform the game into many applications. I want my readers to note the benefits listed below. And as said before, the interests are looked at at a different perspective.

1. Enhancing Data mining

Data mining is the extraction of massive sets of data for analysis and transformation into valuable information. The frequent use of digital information calls for a reliable and competent method of retrieving data from its raw source and state. These methods must generate a large amount of data in the shortest time possible. How fast data analysis and the results are required makes manual processes challenging; thus, machine learning comes in hand.

The functionality of machine learning in the field of data mining is crucial. When incorporated, the method allows for analysis of the large volume of data while providing accurate assumptions that give weight to the outcome at the same time. A point to note is that data mining is the extraction of data, while machine learning is the analysis of the extracted data to make predictions and get accurate results. The two go hand in hand and supplement each other for best outcomes.

2. Enabling continuous improvements and innovation

The term 'learning' from machine learning indicates the ability to improve in knowledge and performance. The general context of learning shows that experience is used to improve future outcomes. In machine learning, the software and algorithmic functions act as agents that will enhance the performance of individual computer systems. I have shown that the algorithm learns sets of data inputs to refine the system they operate in. When a prediction is made, the outcome is stored. If the result is not fitting the users' needs, the algorithms learn to improve their performance the next time such a task is performed.

The ability of machine learning to enable improvements and further innovations can be applied in various fields. For instance, let us take a look at a machine learning algorithm that analyzes the changing patterns of stock prices. The algorithm will not only take into account the past results and data but also look at the newly input features. Such features may include all the factors affecting the market. These factors are analyzed within a specified duration. Machine learning systems are thereby able to make accurate predictions and recommendations.

3. Computerization of tasks

The widely known advantage of machine learning is the automation of tasks. The development of intelligent machine has seen a change in methods of operation. Software and other computer programs are trained to perform the functions that are instead deemed tiresome to human beings. Automation of these processes is made possible by supplementing both data mining and machine learning through constant improvements. Machine learning has undisputedly been developed to perform tasks on their own without any programming commands.

Human functions are complemented well with machine learning systems. It is my take to mention that incorporating machine learning algorithms in one or more tasks would free up humans to focus on more critical issues.

There are notable instances of automating human tasks that are worth a mention. I want to refer you to the applications and uses of machine learning in the chapters above to get a glimpse of the automated tasks. However, I will take a peek on another area in this chapter.

Technology has evolved to the extent that driving and piloting functions can be automated. As an area that did not get massive back up in my opening chapters, I would like to focus a bit here. Drones and crewless planes are an example of automated functions. Human is no longer required to pilot aeroplanes. However, the processes remain controlled by humans on the ground. Nevertheless, a wide range of production sectors and industries are at present, reaping the benefits of machine learning systems. The companies are using the methods to introduce innovations, advance their service delivery mechanisms, and encourageeffectiveness in operations.

These functions have created an opportunity to use fewer people in handling the processes. On the contrary, automation can also be seen as a miss. Many people argue that machines have taken human chances of employment. A human cannot outperform machine in some areas, thereby falling victims of computerization processes. It is, however, important to use devices sparingly and only in fields that human performance is deemed irrelevant.

Limitations of Machine Learning

The wins of machine learning, as discussed above the point at the innovation of systems capable of improving the way processes and tasks are accomplished. However, regardless of the numerous benefits, machine learning processes do not fall short of limitations.The limitations of machine learning are outlined below.

1. The algorithms of Machine Learning are bulky

One of the most notable aspects of machine learning algorithms is bulk. These algorithms require large storage spaces for the training data. It is worth noting that machine learning algorithms and systems are trained and not programmed. The training phases need a lot of data input to train and test the system. The complexity of the tasks makes it even more bulky in terms of the sets of data required to complete the processes.

Contrary to the fact that data is generated at fascinating speed, robust computing power for this performance means that a lot of information is used. In return, the data requires a lot of input space. Large amounts of data are challenging to mine, analyze, and transform into meaningful information. For this reason, deep learning is used to utilizebackpropagation. This algorithmic function enables adjustment of the weights between nodes, thus ensuring that data input corresponds to the right output.

The main limitation with these processes is that machine learning algorithms need too much 'applied features' to perform at the same level as the intelligence level of humans.

However, this limitation can be mitigated by infusing deep learning and unsupervised learning methods. As discussed earlier, we can note that unsupervised learning does not require massive labelled data input for training algorithms. A case in point is that reinforcement learning algorithms are trained through trial and error instead of input data. Using this method would ensure that the massive sets of data are checked.

2. The process of labelling training data is time-consuming

Supervised learning is a fundamental component of machine learning. In supervised learning, the algorithms require labelled datasets for training. The method works efficiently when datasets from previous functions are infused into the system.

The process of data labelling entails cleaning up raw data and sorting it out for machines to gulp down. Machine learning functions, especially in supervised and semi-supervised learning, require large amounts of training data. The process of labelling these sets of training data is not only tiresome but also time-consuming. On the contrary, when unlabeled data is fed in the system, the performance of the machine is lowered. This is down to the fact that algorithms can make decisions, recognize, and behave intelligently only if mapped targets are made available.

A time-wasting and tedious process of identifying and labelling training data are required to establish the targets. A point of relief is that developers are coming up with new means of identifying and labelling training data that may not be as time-consuming as the existing methods. The developments in this area include adding features to the system that would naturally develop the training data. The innovation not only promises to upgrade the quality of data collection but also save the users time and energy required to do so.

3. Machines do not offer explanations

The human brain has an insightful physics engine. This means that the human brain is capable of collect information in all sorts of environment and makes conclusions of the outcome of the collected data. Well, thought explanations can back the findings. One of the most limiting factors of machine learning is the inability of the machine to give insights about the outcome generated. In other terms, computers are not capable of backing up their decisions with explanations. For ages now, devices have continued to exhibit a lack of common sense. Many models of machine learning depend on the availability of training data. Such circumstances have primarily resulted in a lack of receptiveness in machine learning in fields that require explanations. Social processes have the right to descriptions. Whether the results are bad or good, we at time demand to know why and how the decisions are made. The understanding of the outcome is very crucial in knowing how the systems operate. The knowledge can be used to understand mechanical machines and their models as well as the modes of operation.

4. Machine Learning algorithms are prone to bias

Anysystem that relies on the deployment of information by a human is usually likely to prejudice. Partiality comes in the order at the point of feeding input data for training. Humans may tend to shift the machine operations to fit their need. In some cases, systems that seem to perform effectively manage to operate on "noisy data."The reliability of machine learning processes is dependent on the data input. This means that when the information is bias, the result may not reflect the actual value on the ground. The best way to overcome bias is by collecting data randomly from numerous sources. An assortment of data limits the exposure of the data to prejudice, thus ensuring accurate outcomes.

5. Machine Learning Algorithms do not collaborate

Despite numerous improvements in machine learning, the systems continue to show an inability to generalize factors within their environment. That is to say thatthose machines fail to apply the knowledge in different cases. The models of machine learning find transferring experience from one problem to the other a challenge. Machine learning algorithms can only perform a task they have trained to do. As a result of this limitation, many users are forced to put their resources in training different algorithms to perform various tasks. A situation that requires a lot of investments.

To solve this problem, users and developers need to learn how to transfer training. Transfer learning means that a model is fed with input data that reflects a possible problem and other related problems. From this process, the know-how acquired from solving one problem can be used for a similar problem without further training.

Points to note on the benefits and limitations of Machine Learning

The above-mentioned hits and misses of machine learning do not portray the general scope of the process. It is worth noting that different methods are used to build and train the algorithms.The pros and cons all depend on the techniques in which the models are developed, deployed and trained. Additionally, the limitations of machine learning rely on the problems to be solved and the software that they are built-in. Lastly, it is essential to note that the wins and losses are dependent on the quality of input data.

Conclusion

The last couples of years have witnessed amazing breakthroughs in the field of artificial intelligence and its branch; machine learning. In this era, machines can learn and act like humans while performing various tasks. The innovations in machine learning have enabled experts to build tools that can mimic multi-dimensional functions such as making decisions, reasoning deductively and making inferences. Robotics is no longer considered science fiction. The reality in the ground is that the concept of machine learning has evolved to an unimaginable extent. Today, human society is more dependent on the complement of machines in making decisions and solving their daily problems. Multiple industries have embraced the incorporations of intelligent machines in their production practices. As indicated in the chapters above, machine learning application has become a part of human life. And as Sundar Pichai would put it, the use of machine learning in human life is more intense than electricity and fire.

However, it is good to understand that these uses have evolved to cover deep learning and other areas of artificial intelligence completely. The coverage has enabled algorithms to perform complex tasks with noteworthy inferences for the way production methods are run, giving results in the least possible time. In all the buildup that surrounds this fantastic field of technological study, the integrity that gets lost is that machine learning, like any other field, has its limitations. Machine learning technology requires considerable effort to overcome the hurdles and advance in scope. My opinion, therefore, is that my readers should try the different models and note the ones suitable for their course. For academic purposes, learners should juggle books that touch on basics of all branches of artificial intelligence.

www.ingramcontent.com/pod-product-compliance
Lightning Source LLC
Chambersburg PA
CBHW070834070326
40690CB00009B/1548